How to Do Psychotherapy and How to Evaluate It

A MANUAL FOR BEGINNERS

John Mordechai Gottman, *Indiana University*
Sandra Risa Leiblum, *Rutgers Medical School*

With preface by
Leonard Ullmann
University of Hawaii

HOLT, RINEHART AND WINSTON, INC.
New York Chicago San Francisco Atlanta
Dallas Montreal Toronto London Sydney

To Richard McFall,
my colleague and teacher.

John M. Gottman

To Leonard Ullmann,
a gentle man, whose contributions as a
teacher, friend, and advisor I will not
forget. He tempers wisdom with kindness,
professional leadership with humanity,
and unfailing generosity with judgment.

Sandra R. Leiblum

Library of Congress Cataloging in Publication Data

Gottman, John Mordechai.
How to do psychotherapy and how to evaluate it.

(Person in psychology series)
1. Psychotherapy. I. Leiblum, Sandra Risa, joint author. II. Title.
[DNLM: 1. Psychotherapy. WM420 G686h 1974]
RC480.5.G64   616.8'914   73-16978

ISBN: 0-03-007651-X

FOREWORD

CONTEMPORARY CLASSROOM TEACHERS of psychology place a high value on diversity when they select reading materials for their students. University and college teachers like to choose from among full coverage textbooks, anthologies, journal articles, and small books that focus on specific topics. While there is an abundance of textbooks, anthologies, and journal articles, the supply of small topical books is limited. To meet the need for small textbooks that deal with important aspects of the study of persons, the Person in Psychology series was established.

The series is devoted to in-depth reporting of relevant subjects which are frequently included in college courses with such titles as: "Personality," "Socialization," "The Individual and Society," "Stress and Adaptation," "Personality and Culture," "Clinical Psychology," and "Personality and Adjustment."

In selecting topics for the series, the editor has tried to steer a middle course between overly broad areas of study such as "Motivation," or "Cognition," and highly specialized themes such as "Child-Rearing Patterns in Three Island Communities" or "Bargaining Behavior among Ghetto Youth." "Cognition," on the one hand, is too broad a topic for a small book; on the other hand, "Bargaining Behavior among Ghetto Youth," while timely, is too specific for most undergraduate courses. The titles of the books published thus far indicate the not-too-broad, not-too-narrow concept of the series. They are: *Beliefs and Values* (by Karl E. Scheibe), *Aggression and Altruism* (by Harry Kaufmann), *The Concept of Self* (by Kenneth A. Gergen), and *Sex and Identity* (B. G. Rosenberg and B. Sutton-Smith).

How to Do Psychotherapy and How to Evaluate It is a welcome addition to the series. Professors Gottman and Leiblum have written a step-by-step account that will inform not only the beginner but also the experienced practitioner. The strategic use of flow chart and down-to-earth language helps remove much of the mystification that has traditionally surrounded the acquisition of therapeutic skills. Their exposition of the need for continuing evaluation of the therapeutic enterprise and their proposals for engaging in systematic evaluation will serve as guides to the novice and will act as constant reminders to the master therapist that psychotherapy without systematic evaluation is incomplete psychotherapy.

The authors besides being specialists in clinical psychology are also teachers of undergraduates, and therefore are sensitive to the needs of contemporary students. This book is written from the perspective that the student is the primary reader, not the professional colleague or the professor in some distant university. Even a cursory examination will convince the reader that the book is oriented to undergraduate students. Professors Gottman and Leiblum tell it like it is.

University of California   Theodore R. Sarbin
Santa Cruz   *General Editor*

iii

PREFACE

*I*F PSYCHOLOGICAL GROWTH is defined as an increasing ability to cope effectively and productively with one's environment, then this book is a growth experience. It draws from and together many traditions while maintaining the ideal of the therapist as a scientist and teacher as well as professional. Social learning, systems analysis, role theory, and behavioral analysis mingle in a consistent fashion and replace reliance on medical model, personality dynamics, and therapy process rather than therapy outcome.

The book is written for the beginning therapist, but not for a person without psychological sophistication. The reader is presumed to know some basic psychology and to be prepared to follow up references for further explication. While there is useful detail, the procedures and forms are explicitly starting points. The authors provide a guidebook and some cogent leads to travels in the land of psychotherapy, but they do not free the therapist from his obligation to think for himself. No volume or system can or should replace the individual therapist's obligation to be sensitive, flexible, creative, and selective in fitting methods to the needs and abilities of his client. Further, procedures are always used with people, and people vary both among each other and within themselves as they change. The object for both therapist and client lies not in a set of responses, but in appropriate responses to many different situations. This book should be used as a guide and as a start, not as a final, finished product.

This volume also is one of the small, but fortunately increasing, number of attempts by therapists to specify what they are doing, not in high-flown, mystical terms, but in language that can be used where it counts, in the treatment situation. While intended as an aid to the starting therapist, the outline permits the maturing clinician to integrate his insights. One can only hope for revisions, extensions, and ever more accurate specification of terms, procedures, and rationales.

Clearly written, scientifically sound, yet human and at times humorous, this all too brief book is a genuine accomplishment. It helps; and there is nothing better one can say about the work of therapists.

Leonard P. Ullmann
University of Hawaii
Honolulu

AUTHORS' PREFACE

*T*WO IMPORTANT POINTS motivated us to prepare this book. The first is our belief that psychotherapy needs to be based on a scientific epistemology. This means that therapy needs to be empirically grounded and that the therapist needs to be a scientist. We do not mean that the therapist should merely have research training, but that he should be a scientist *while* he is doing therapy. We therefore feel that the evaluation of therapy is essential. By "evaluation" we mean the continuous monitoring of progress toward goals. The data should be used as feedback to make decisions about the effectiveness of intervention components of the treatment program. This is important to us as therapists because it capitalizes on the potential learning we can get from experience.

Second, we feel that a methodology is needed to individualize psychotherapy and its evaluation. We concur with Lazarus (1971) who stated in his preface that

> the intent of this book is to caution therapists and would-be therapists not to forget the obvious fact that every individual is unique, and to tailor his therapy accordingly. (p. *xi*)

For that reason we have proposed a graphical method of single-subject monitoring called time-series analysis. This method permits the statistical assessment of change in the single case.

We have tried to be systematic in writing a "how to" book that attends to the current research literature on psychotherapy. Again, we agreed with Lazarus (1971) who offered:

> . . . an antipanacea approach . . . not for or against "insight," nor for or against "deconditioning," [but] concerned with the combination of techniques which seems likely to be most beneficial to the people who ask for help. (p. *xii*)

We decided to write this book during a postdoctoral year at the University of Colorado Medical Center; we are thankful for that learning experience. We each sampled a wide array of clinical situations, ranging from work in a children's day treatment educational setting to an adult in-patient psychiatric ward. Often, we came together to exchange, synthesize, and understand our experiences. It was during one of these times that we decided to consolidate our learning. Having grappled with a multitude of issues facing the clinician and planning a career of training others, we wanted to share what worked for us in the hope that it might stimulate discussion.

There are many people we would like to thank. Richard McFall's thinking patterns have geared our own minds to action. His careful and constructive criticism of the manuscript has been invaluable. We would like to thank Leonard Ullmann for his helpful suggestions and emotional support. We are also grateful to Gene Glass and Jean and Marty Goldsmith for reading the manuscript and providing helpful suggestions. We would like to acknowledge Karen Craig for her work on the index. Professors Fredrick Todd and Robert Kelley (now of the Behavior Therapy Institute of Colorado) were helpful and encouraging during our first draft of the book. Ruth Hartman typed and improved the first draft of the manuscript. She also introduced us to our publishers, Holt, Rinehart and Winston. Thanks, Ruth. Donna Littrell, Diane Rodgers, and Judy Jerkich patiently and speedily typed and retyped the next umpteen drafts. We would also like to thank Ted Sarbin, Deborah Doty, and Johnna Barto for their work on the manuscript. Finally, Gottman would like to thank his wife Heidi who continues to provide the meaning for his whole show.

Bloomington, Indiana   J. M. G.
New Brunswick, New Jersey   S. R. L.
December 1973

CONTENTS

Introduction

THIS BOOK IS DESIGNED for the inexperienced, would-be psychotherapist. It is an attempt to help the student obtain an overview of the process and evaluation of psychotherapy and reduce the inevitable worry and self-doubt we all experience when starting out. We believe that one of the greatest sources of worry to the novice therapist is the absence of a meaningful conceptual framework. Caught in the raging war between dynamicists and behaviorists, the beginning therapist may find himself a neutral, befuddled onlooker. We have attempted to provide a viable way of specifying what we believe psychotherapy is and have made suggestions for doing psychotherapy. More importantly, we have also attempted to provide a guide for evaluating the process and product of psychotherapy.

We intend our conceptualization as a guide for the student to react to. Hopefully our system will produce discussion since our aim is to stimulate the student to generate his own ideas. We have learned that students find it helpful to react to (or against) some framework.

There are many reasons why it has seemed difficult to teach people how to do psychotherapy. A major obstacle has been the reluctance of many therapists to define psychotherapy and to specify what it is that the therapist needs to do to carry out psychotherapy. Some therapists are pleased to say that psychotherapy cannot "really" be defined, that it is an elusive, intuitive process. We do not deny that there is some truth in that feeling. But we also feel that the intuitive can be defined; the desire to do so is a question of aesthetics. The process of evaluation demands specificity of techniques and goals.

Any book that attempts to be specific about psychotherapy is likely to please some people and to disturb many others because goals vary, as do methods. Mahrer (1967) compiled an interesting collection of discussions on the goals of psychotherapy. Some writers have proposed that psychotherapy should be designed to help individuals adjust; others have suggested that psychotherapy may be employed to create a new social order (Skinner, 1971), or "the new man" (Maslow, 1962).

We have tried to specify what psychotherapy is. Figure 1 is a flow chart of psychotherapy that outlines the treatment process. Quite a number of things that others call psychotherapy will not fit our flow chart. That does not mean that we

1

think these things are not valuable, important, or effective. A religious experience, for example, may be intensely meaningful and change-producing for an individual. Although we may acknowledge this, we will not discuss all such processes. Some practicing therapists may agree in principle with the flow chart but emphasize some sections of it more than others. That is fine. Our hope is to provide a conceptual road map for the student of therapy, and our goals are humble. We trust that this book will be a valuable working contribution to your library. We certainly do not intend to replace your library or discourage you from adding to it. In fact, we will often refer you to sources that we think you will find helpful.

Let us state, however, that we do intend to provide you with some things you will not find in other books. We believe that once psychotherapy has been specified, it becomes possible to evaluate its progress. Too often, evaluation is done by consensus among professionals involved with the case when treatment terminates. Occasionally, such evaluations speculate about the crucial factors responsible for a patient's improvement. However, we believe that evaluation should take place continuously during the course of treatment and that it is needed to provide the client and therapist with feedback so that decisions are not made in an informational vacuum. Our hope, then, is to link the practice of psychotherapy with the investigation of psychotherapy to pursue therapeutic goals.

We realize that many therapists are about as interested in the evaluation of psychotherapy as they are in having someone else judge the quality of their lovemaking. If this attitude is due to an ubiquitous fear and distaste for research and statistics, numbers and equations, and the symbol paralysis many people experience when the term "research" is uttered, then we can help. We think we have a methodology to propose that will make evaluation sensible and accessible to the nonstatistician. Hopefully this methodology will make both the practice and investigation of psychotherapy more scientific, more interesting, and more effective.

It should be pointed out that we are working from what we think is a cognitive-behavioral framework. Much of our terminology is behavioral. We consider ourselves to be natural scientists as well as psychotherapists. Some of our language is cognitive, some smacks of psychodynamic conceptualizations, and some is oriented by systems analysis. The very choice of terminology, we realize, may unfortunately reduce our audience. This is sad, but probably unavoidable. We hope the reader will borrow and choose from our presentation according to his needs. It is our intention to include only those concepts which we feel are practical for the beginning therapist.

Experience tells us that students find the step-by-step conceptualization of psychotherapy useful. Initial therapy sessions are often frustrating to the beginner who does not see any significant change in the presenting problem. It is important to recognize that work preliminary to structured intervention efforts needs to be done in order to formulate the problem, establish a therapeutic alliance, and strike a contract.

In summary, this book is designed to provide:

1. a conceptual framework for the practice of psychotherapy,
2. an evaluation procedure for the ongoing process and outcome of therapy, employing continuous feedback, and
3. a step-by-step flow chart specifying the major techniques and requirements of each stage.

A WALK THROUGH THE FLOW CHART

This book will take you through the flow chart in Figure 1 step by step. Each chapter of the book will explain and discuss issues connected to a particular part of the flow chart, illustrate the discussion with case material, and suggest references helpful in clarifying or elaborating that particular aspect of therapy. Let us reiterate that this flow chart is offered with modesty, as a framework around which the beginning therapist can mold his own ideas.

You will notice that the flow chart falls into roughly five parts. The first part involves the initial assessment of the problem (which may change). The second part involves the formation of the therapeutic contract between the therapist and client (or client system). The third part involves initial change efforts. The fourth part involves interventions to deal with the client's possible resistance to behavior change. The fifth part involves the continuous monitoring of change and eventual follow-up.

Let us take a more detailed look at the flow chart.

A. In the beginning stages of assessment the therapist will have to decide whom to see during the assessment phase. A whole family may be involved, or parts of it in various configurations; the school may be involved; other significant people and institutions entering into the presenting problem may be involved. When seeing an individual client it may be necessary to see the client's co-workers, roommates, boyfriend, or girl friend. If the client is an organization or part of an organization, it may be necessary to designate those components of the organizational system which need to be involved in the problem assessment. We call this "designating the organizational system."

Example: Mr. and Mrs. Schmedlap came in for therapy. Mr. Schmedlap was a graduate student. They proposed that their problems were primarily marital although Mr. Schmedlap complained of difficulty in organizing his time and in systematically preparing for his doctoral examination. They agreed that there were no problems in the area of raising their son. Mr. Schmedlap felt that it would be helpful if we spoke to his advisor and felt that his advisor would be willing to speak to us.

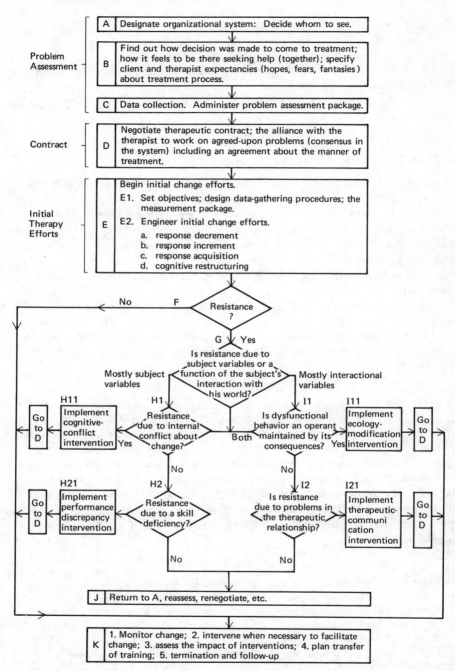

Figure 1. Flow chart of psychotherapy.

B. How the decision was made to come for treatment provides the therapist with important information. In a family it can provide hunches about habitual patterns of communication. The therapist will have to deal with the issues of whether help is voluntarily sought, and how it feels and what it means to be seeking help. In an organizational system the mere coming together may have serious implications that need to be explored. Client and therapist expectations of treatment, the client's hopes, fears, and fantasies, as well as concepts of what the treatment will be like need to be examined. The decision of whether to refer the client elsewhere may need to be made at this point.

Example: The Bowen family urged the therapist to speak to each of them individually before holding meetings with the family as a group. They felt that they each could say things that would seriously hurt other family members, but they thought the therapist should know about these things so he would not probe too deeply in some specific areas. They were afraid the therapist had the power to root out these feelings against their will.

C. The therapist will *then* want to get to the problem itself, and an analysis of the problem in terms that are helpful in prescribing treatment. For this stage there are a great many options open. Psychological testing, different kinds of interviews, and behavioral assessment are discussed. We then present a problem assessment package that we feel has a reasonable degree of utility (that is, you get a lot of information at low cost) and applicability with a variety of clients.

Example: With Mr. and Mrs. Schmedlap it was determined that there were marital problems in the areas of sex and communication and that Mr. Schmedlap needed help in organizing his studying for his examination and in structuring his time. After a series of interviews, the therapists listed all the couple's problem areas and specific situations that exemplified these problem areas. The therapists obtained play-by-plays (who said what) in these situations and listed dysfunctional (conflict reducing but not conflict resolving) communication patterns which prevented the couple from reaching agreements in these situations.

D. The therapist will then negotiate a therapeutic contract with the client or client system to work on agreed-upon problems in a specified manner. The contract may involve ending the therapeutic relationship, referral elsewhere if this seems most appropriate, or continuing treatment with the therapist. The therapist will need to consider setting ground rules and fees for treatment at this point.

Example: The therapists wrote a problem assessment summary report for Mr. and Mrs. Schmedlap in which they listed the problems and specified the treatment they recommended for each problem.

E. Initial behavior change efforts are then begun. These involve some combination of understanding and clarifying perceptions (which include exploration of the client's characteristic ways of thinking, construing experience, and generating alternatives), or, changing responses (decreasing the frequency of an inappropriate response or increasing the frequency of an appropriate response). It may also be necessary to modify the client's ecology, that is to say, the people (or systems) that maintain, reinforce, or extinguish the client's response (both appropriate and inappropriate). In this stage specific goals and subgoals need to be set, data gathering procedures for getting feedback on how psychotherapy is progressing need to be designed, and the specific tasks of initial change efforts need to be delineated.

> *Example:* Three major interventions were agreed upon for the problems specified. For sexual problems it was agreed that the Masters and Johnson program would be undertaken, but only after communication patterns improve as indicated by the couple's successful resolution of two unresolved problem situations. For Mr. Schmedlap's studying problems, one of the therapists acted as a study skills counselor and taught Mr. Schmedlap a method called P.E.R.T. (Archibald and Villoria, 1968). A faculty member in his department also agreed to meet with him to go over his answers to old examination questions. For the couple's communication problems a contingency contracting approach (Stuart, 1969) was used. The couple attempted to negotiate contracted agreements at home about problem areas such as the housework tasks. They were given a cassette tape recorder to use and they taped their conversations at home. The therapists then went over these tapes in therapy and made suggestions for improving communication, using coaching and role-playing alternative ways of arriving at a solution in a problem situation.

F. We define resistance as occurring when the client(s) is not meeting the therapist's expectations regarding "meaningful, goal-oriented therapeutic work." Resistance is a description of certain kinds of overt or covert verbalizations and actions made by the client, and not an explanation of lack of progress. There are many reasons why initial change efforts do not appear to be working or, are not being actively implemented by the client. The therapist's expectations may need to be reexamined. Often, initial change efforts serve the function of bringing the therapist and client to the first line of defense against change. Resistance may also be information the client is giving the therapist to change his initial therapy efforts.

G. Resistance can be very roughly categorized as involving either those things that the client typically brings with him in interacting with his world (his skills, thoughts, and feelings) or the way in which the ecology responds to the client's characteristic patterns.

H1. Resistance may be due to cognitive and/or affective implications of the change for the client or client system. Internal conflicts and ambivalence about change must be explored as obstacles to intervention efforts. In Section H11, the use of psychological interpretation is discussed to alter what Kelly (1955) called the client's personal construct system. Psychological interpretation is discussed from Levy's (1963) viewpoint.

H2. Resistance may be due to the client's inability to behave in ways the therapist feels are desirable. This may require a training program so that the client may develop necessary skills. Alternatively, the therapist may reconsider his own expectations of the "good patient" role and consider therapeutic procedures that utilize a client's competencies and available response patterns. If the therapist decides to adopt a training program, Unit H21 will suggest guidelines for writing a program reducing the discrepancy between the therapist's expectations and the client's performance. This intervention is discussed in connection with the response acquisition model of behavior change (McFall and Marston, 1970; McFall and Twentyman, 1973).

GO TO D. After each intervention, the therapist is sent back to D to check on the relevancy of the therapeutic contract. The trip to D may be a formality or an important renegotiation of the contract which in turn leads to a new change program at E.

I1. Resistance or lack of therapeutic movement may be traced to the discovery that the rewards and payoffs in the client's environment are designed to elicit and maintain the dysfunctional behavior. The client may have no alternative methods for obtaining desired payoffs. The therapist needs to consider modifying the environment by changing reinforcement contingencies, discriminative cues eliciting behavior, and/or teaching the client alternative functional ways of obtaining the rewarding consequences (I11). The question can be rephrased as, "Is resistance due to systems norms which act to resist change?" The only gain in rephrasing the question in this way is that it involves the terminology of communications theory which may give the therapist a different conceptual handle on modifications of the social psychology of the systems which resist the client's change.

I2. Resistance may be due to problems in communication between client and therapist. Unit I21 is a discussion of the issues of affection, inclusion, status, and control that may be involved. The therapeutic relationship is viewed as a social influence process (Goldstein, Heller, and Sechrest, 1966) in Unit I21. Concepts of transference (client's reaction to the therapist) and countertransference (the therapist's reaction to the client) are also discussed in Unit I21.

J. If resistance still exists, it may be useful to return to A, decide again about whom to include in the treatment process, reassess the problem (B and C), and renegotiate the therapeutic contract (D).

K. If change efforts are succeeding, it is important to monitor change, reinforce it, and intervene when necessary to facilitate change. We are suggesting the use of time-series designs to assess the impact of planned interventions in the single case.

Example: The Schmedlaps were asked to buy pocket golf counters which allow the counting of two kinds of events at once. Since the major objective in this case was to improve the marital communication, they were instructed to tally "putts" and "strokes." A stroke was defined as something done by the spouse that was enjoyable or pleasant; a putt as something unpleasant. The objective of treatment was to improve communication so that strokes increased significantly to a level the Schmedlaps both found desirable and putts decreased significantly to a level they both found acceptable. Total daily putts and strokes were graphed over time. "Checkups" one and six months after termination will involve interviews with the Schmedlaps to ascertain how they report things going. The Schmedlaps are still in treatment at the time of this writing

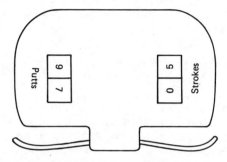

A crude but useful graphical method is discussed in the text and the reader is referred to the appendix for a more sophisticated method using a computer program. The evaluation strategy also includes two systematic methods for generating hypotheses: (1) the annotated record, and (2) the study of concommitant variation.

The therapist also needs to deal with an important and neglected aspect of psychotherapy—transfer of training. We do not suggest that transfer is programmed only at the end of treatment. It must be an integral part of the entire psychotherapy process.

Finally, we discuss issues of termination and follow-up.

That was a brief walk through the flow chart. We hope we have generated many questions by this presentation and that some of them will be answered in the rest of the book. Examples are used in this book to illustrate our discussion. They are usually based upon real cases, but at times are fictional. Fictional cases are indicated. We should say a word about our examples. Many of them have successful outcomes; but that does not mean that we have always succeeded. The best claim we can make is we learn a bit from failure.

THE COMPETENCE-INCOMPETENCE "ROLLER COASTER"

Like most therapists, we have been up and down the same emotional coaster. After some sessions we have come out "high" on ourselves as therapists, exhilarated by the experience and feeling confident about our abilities. At other times (perhaps the next session with the same client) we have come out feeling like we did not know what we were doing, down in the dumps about our own incompetence. We may have been unable to think of what to say the whole hour. We have each said to ourselves (and meant it) after such sessions, "Well, maybe I'm in the wrong field." If you find yourselves on this roller coaster you ought to ask yourself that question too, but you need to recognize that people who are now considered capable therapists were on the same roller coaster once. All we can say is that it does get better; experience does help. We believe the best help comes from having systematic procedures for learning from our failures as well as our successes.

I

Designate Organizational System: Decide Whom to See

A. Designate organizational system: decide whom to see

GEORGE KELLY (1955) called attention to the fact that the process of labeling behavior as deviant occurs in a social context. If a psychologist calls a child a giraffe, you would be more likely to look strangely at the psychologist, not at the child. But if a psychologist calls a child hyperactive, you may be likely to look more closely at the child. In the initial stages of therapy the presenting problem must be viewed in the systems in which complaints have arisen. This may make it necessary to investigate several behavior settings (for example, in a child therapy case the home and the classroom might be studied) to identify the people in each setting concerned with the problem and to study the labels they apply.

Labels applied by observers frequently describe a presenting problem in terms of what a person *has* or does not have rather than in terms of what a person *does*. For example, a teacher in a classroom will describe a child in terms of how much attention span he has rather than describing what he does in specific situations that are disturbing.

Research evidence suggests that trait and state labels based upon an underlying assumption of generalized response dispositions do not predict behavior well (Mischel, 1968). There is a good deal of situational specificity to human behavior; prediction is best from one situation to behavior in similar situations (Bandura, 1969). This has important implications for the psychotherapist. For example, Patterson, Cobb, and Ray (1971) reported that modifying children's behavior problems in the home often does not solve behavior problems in school, and vice versa. Each behavior setting had to be studied separately for interventions to be effective, although a coordinated program was found to be most effective by these investigators.

Another pitfall of the trait or state label is that it appears to provide an *explanation* for the behavior whereas it represents only a renaming. A child is said to fight children *because* he has a lot of aggression, or is functioning poorly in intellectual tasks *because* he has less intelligence than other children. An adjective describing a behavior often becomes real, or "reified," by making it a noun and then equipping the noun with an animistic power to explain causally the initial behavior. The process of looking for internal causal agents has led therapists to ignore situational variables. As Bandura (1969) aptly stated,

> Preoccupation with internal response-producing agents has resulted in a disregard of external variables that have nevertheless been shown to exercise control over behavior. (p. 19)

The therapist can sometimes obtain valuable information by studying the labeling process in the human systems in which it occurs. An example of this is the "identified patient phenomenon" in family treatment (Satir, 1964). Let us consider the labeling process in the context of the family system.

The identified patient in a family is that member of the family who is perceived by all family members as THE PROBLEM. At times, this may be quite true: A particularly healthy family may have a child who presents problems.

Example: Mr. and Mrs. Blount requested help because their six-year-old son, Paul, was disruptive to his class at school. The teacher complained that Paul was a "hyperactive child" who required constant attention. The Blounts said they were not certain whether Paul was a problem at home since he was their first child and they had no other children to compare him with. They were, however, surprised by the teacher's comments and noted that Paul would "amuse himself for hours at a time at home without being a bother." They did say that Paul was an energetic child who could be annoying at times. They came to the clinic at the teacher's suggestion to inquire about the use of "special" drugs to reduce Paul's hyperactivity.

The therapist decided to observe Paul in class. It was noted that Paul was most disruptive during "story time" when he would run around the room, shouting, waving his arms, and making silly faces. Paul's teacher dealt with this by holding him on her lap, explaining to the therapist that "this is the only way I can calm him down and get his full attention." It seemed as though Paul had successfully trained his teacher to reward his disruptive behavior with special privileges and extraordinary attention. When she was helped to focus on Paul's appropriate behavior and reward it with attention, and ignore Paul's classroom antics, the problem subsided and eventually disappeared.

Often, the identified patient is an indication of a problem in the family itself. A child may be brought to a clinic so that his parents have a legitimate reason for requesting (directly or indirectly) help for themselves.

Example: Mr. and Mrs. Winston complained that seven-year-old Kathy was constantly engaged in attention-seeking behavior. She would tease her younger brother, tantalize the puppy, and nag her parents whenever they were discussing something. The therapist decided to see the family together in order to obtain a clearer idea of what conditions triggered Kathy's attention-seeking behavior. Careful observation revealed that whenever Mr. and Mrs. Winston began arguing about money and in-laws (which was frequent!), Kathy got going. By focusing attention onto herself, she disrupted her parents' battles and enabled them to come together in agreement about Kathy. When this was pointed out to the Winstons, they said that they were experiencing marital difficulties and inquired about help for themselves.

A third possibility is that the "identified patient" does have problems but that treatment must occur in the family or marital system in order for treatment to be effective.

Example: Mrs. Billings called the outpatient clinic complaining of her frequent depressions. She added that she had been "down in the dumps" ever since her family moved recently. Throughout the telephone conversation, Mrs. Billings' references to her husband were made in an irritated tone, though her words were rather neutral. The therapist decided to see Mr. and Mrs. Billings together to assess the problem. When the topic of the recent move came up, the therapist asked how the decision to move had been made. Mrs. Billings declared that she had not been consulted at all. Mr. Billings blithely disregarded his wife's anger and wanted to focus on her "depressions."

It became apparent by the end of the session that the depression was related to dysfunctional communication within the marriage and communication difficulties became the focus of psychotherapy.

In any organizational system, be it a family, group, marriage, or a work team, each member will have different perceptions of the "real problem" in that system. The very fact of coming together in your office as a group to deal with a problem may represent a serious threat. For example, many families can tolerate only a certain amount of "closeness." These families do not even dine together in order to avoid upsetting a tenuous family equilibrium. In an organization that seeks consulting help, the staff members may be afraid of being open because they think it will jeopardize smooth working relationships or even job security.

To clarify and understand what the problem is in any particular system, it is often useful to see the system in various combinations. For example, parents may be more willing to discuss sexual difficulties in the absence of their children; children may express concerns about their alcoholic father or promiscuous mother or their private "worries" more easily without their parents present. If the client system is a school system, administrators, teachers, students, and community members may be seen separately in order to understand the different concerns of these groups and in various combinations to explore problem areas in the functioning of the organizational system.

However, splitting up any system for problem assessment can have serious consequences. The issue of confidentiality needs to be dealt with whenever parts of an organization are seen separately. For example, if a social worker sees the parents and a psychologist sees the child (or vice versa), each therapist will probably develop loyalty toward his own client. The psychologist may tell the social worker, "Do something about these terrible parents" and the social worker may reply, "Get that kid off their backs so they can have some peace." Alternatively, if the family is seen as a unit, the therapist must be sensitive to family "secrets" and games, absent-member syndromes (in which the person absent that session gets attacked and scapegoated), and each member's individual defensive maneuvers. It is essential when treating a family to find out how they would like to be seen and their fears and concerns about being offered treatment together. At times, it may be necessary to change the constellation of people seen in order to facilitate progress. Parents may be seen alone at times, or a mother and daughter combination, or father and son, or father and daughter, and so on. Different material will often emerge as a consequence of different family groupings.

While the preceding examples illustrate how important it is for the clinician to be sensitive to the "system" aspects affecting psychological distress, it is often the case that a single individual comes requesting help for himself (or herself). Often, the client's problem may be conceptualized in terms of a performance discrepancy (see Section C of the flow chart). Even when dealing with an individual who designates himself as the source and sole recipient of his difficulties, we encourage the therapist to consider what effects the client's friends, family, and work situation contribute to his current functioning.

In designating "whom to see" in treatment, flexibility is a top priority. At any stage in therapy, it may be useful to change the structure and have "invited" sessions which include significant individuals in the client's life.

Here is a summary of our discussion of Section A in terms of what to *do* at this stage of the problem assessment.

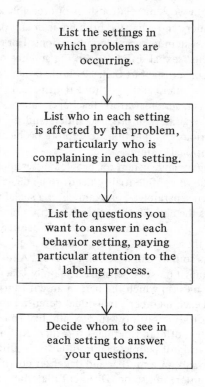

Figure 1.1.   Summary flow chart for Section A.

II

Find Out How
the Decision Was Made
to Come for Treatment

B. Find our how the decision was made to come for treatment; how it feels to be there (together); specify client and therapist expectancies regarding the treatment process.

THE DECISION TO COME FOR TREATMENT

MELTZOFF AND KORNREICH'S (1970) review of research in psychotherapy concluded that "initial motivation is not a *necessary* requirement for improvement" (p. 250). Initial motivation for treatment does, however, seem likely to influence what the therapist does in psychotherapy. It may particularly affect the negotiation of a therapeutic contract (Section D of the flow chart). Many clients *decide* to seek psychotherapy but clients are sometimes referred for psychotherapy by some agency or person who has labeled them as deviant. Usually this means the client's behavior has become sufficiently bothersome to other people so that they are willing to take action. The client may be described as "disturbed" because his behavior is disturbing. The problem in therapy arises from the fact that these are involuntary clients. They are not complaining about discomfort caused by their behavior.

Although some therapists vigorously assert that therapy should not be initiated with a client who does not voluntarily seek it, such an option is not always possible. For example, court-referrals, institutionalized delinquents, autistic children, acutely psychotic persons, and suicidal individuals may all be referred for treatment in institutional settings. One can argue that to refrain from attempting to engage them in treatment is a dereliction of professional responsibility.

Glasser (1965) discussed the problems associated with beginning therapy with institutionalized, delinquent girls who are assigned to "treatment" against their will. In his description of "reality therapy," Glasser reported the initial encounters the therapist had with girls who refused to participate in the treatment program. Such girls were assigned to a "discipline cottage" with minimal privileges. The therapist visited the girl, telling her that he wished to become an ally in helping her get out of the institution. He made his aid contingent on her agreement to participate actively in the program. A situation was thus created in which the alternative to participation (the boredom of the discipline cottage) was the more aversive. Despite this, Glasser reported the action of girls to come to therapy as a "responsible choice."

Anna Freud (1964) discussed the unique problem of striking a therapeutic alliance with a child.

> But what constitutes an even greater difficulty is that in many cases the child itself is not the sufferer, for it often does not perceive the trouble in itself at all; only the persons round it suffer from its symptoms or outbreaks of naughtiness. And so the situation lacks everything which seems indispensible in the case of an adult: insight into the malady, voluntary decision, and the will towards cure . . . it seems that one ought to try whether one cannot produce in the child's case, too, the situation which has proved so favourable in the adults, that is to say, whether one cannot induce in the child in some way the missing readiness and willingness.
>
> I shall make it the subject of my first lecture to show you how in six different cases, of ages between six and eleven, I succeeded in making the small patient "analysable" in the sense of the adult, that is to say inducing an insight into the trouble, imparting confidence in the analyst, and turning the decision for analysis from one taken by others into its own (p. 6).

Many child therapists begin treatment with children by asking the child why he thinks he was brought to treatment and what he expects will happen to him. Often, to allay a child's nervousness, the parents are asked to explain why the child is there or the therapist will explain that he is a "talking doctor who talks to kids about their troubles and how they feel, but doesn't give shots."

In all these cases, writers have noted that the therapist will have more difficulty in striking a therapeutic alliance if the client has not sought help voluntarily. The therapist explores the client's perception of why he's there, and how he feels to be there. He then establishes himself as the client's agent, allied with the client in an initial effort to understand the client's goals. All this takes place in the initial problem assessment phase before striking a therapeutic contract with the client (Section D).

Reluctant adult clients are even more difficult to treat since they may simply refuse to attend therapy sessions, or if coerced, refuse to speak. There is certainly no sure-fire method of securing the cooperation of the involuntary client. Goldstein (1971) cited studies indicating that modeling procedures directed at enhancing attraction to the therapist are sometimes effective in promoting self-disclosure, particularly with YAVIS clients (that is, clients who are *young, attractive, verbal, intelligent,* and *successful*). Section F of the flow chart deals in greater depth with suggestions for overcoming "resistance" to treatment. The point we are making here is that knowing how the client comes (that is, voluntarily or involuntarily) and what his feelings are about being there provide crucial data for subsequent therapeutic decisions. It is valuable to explore with the client how the decision was made to come for treatment even if the client is voluntarily seeking help.

Example: When asked by the therapist how he had decided to come for therapy, a college freshman said, "When I heard you give that speech, I knew that only you could help me. I thought, 'If only I could be as confident as he is.' " The client viewed the therapist as a charismatic figure he thought he should emulate.

With families, exploring how the decision was made to seek treatment allows the therapist to check out communication styles and techniques the family uses for influencing and convincing each other. It also alerts the therapist to the "therapy skeptics" who may then receive special consideration so that they do not sabotage treatment.

HOW IT FEELS TO BE THERE (TOGETHER)

In a situation where one person, family, or other social system seeks help from another person, there is likely to be a variety of feelings about requesting help. Clients may experience relief, anger, anxiety, sadness, or shame in response to coming for treatment. They may be thinking:

1. Only crazy people come here.
2. Only weak people ask for help.
3. Only inadequate individuals seek mental health help.
4. What will the neighbors think (my spouse or girl friend? my friends? my in-laws? my parents? my employer?) if they discover I am seeking psychotherapeutic help?
5. Can I afford this? Is it a luxury? Will it be worth the money?
6. How long must I come?
7. What is going to happen to me? What will it be like?
8. What are the consequences of revealing my problems? Will I be controlled? Will they discover I am insane and lock me up? Will I become worse?
9. Will I fail at this too?

Example: The client is a twenty-five-year-old male referred for therapy by the division of vocational rehabilitation.

Client: I feel nervous waiting for you outside your office.

Therapist: Does it have anything to do with the fact that there's an in-patient ward at the other end of the hall?

Client: Yes. I remember when I was hospitalized for three days—I'm terrified that you may hospitalize me. I hate being locked up. I'm afraid to tell you about myself. What if you decide I'm insane?

Example: The client is an eight-year-old girl.

Therapist: Do you have any idea why you are here?

Client: Because I am afraid of the dark and I can't sleep, and because I can't concentrate in school.

Therapist: You mean you don't sleep at all?

Client: I have a little light I use to shine around the room. It helps me sleep.

Therapist: What do you look for?

Client: I look for vampires. Do you know there's a boy in my class who makes funny faces and acts crazy?

Therapist: And you sometimes feel silly like that boy when you use your light?

Client: I do. I feel silly.

Therapist: You must think it's silly that you have to come here.

Client: Yes.

One of the central issues in the minds of clients is, "Who is this person? Can I trust him? Will he understand me, like me, be able to help me?" The therapist should expect this "testing out" and "sizing up" process to occur as a natural and inevitable part of initial therapeutic encounters. Some treatment facilities have reported success in matching clients with therapists on personality dimensions. However, Garfield's (1971) review of research on client variables in psychotherapy suggested that currently the findings on matching clients with therapists on the basis of similarity or complimentarity is not definitely related to therapeutic outcome.

Kelly (1955, pp. 575–581) suggested that during the course of therapy the therapist should continually ask himself in which role the client is casting him. Kelly suggested that throughout therapy this role may change. Kelly's experience suggested that the client may see the therapist as "a parent, a protector, an absolver of guilt, an authority figure, a prestige figure, a stabilizer, a temporary respite, a threat, an ideal companion, a stooge, or a representative of reality."

When couples or families are seen together, it is essential to understand what it means for the family's homeostasis to be coming together for help. For some families, the expectation of painful things being said, of the power of words, of old wounds being reopened, of carefully kept secrets being revealed may be paramount issues.

> *Example:* The King family was seen together for an initial interview. Mr. and Mrs. King began the interview by attacking their son, complaining of his insubordination and hostility. Fifteen-year-old James sat sullenly while his parents talked about him. When given the opportunity to defend himself, he accused his parents of over-protectiveness and tyranny. He said he was thwarted whenever he wanted to see his friends privately or leave the house after school. "They treat me like an infant!" he declared angrily. When the therapist suggested family meetings on a regular basis, all of the Kings agreed that family meetings were "impossible." "We can't talk together," they each said. Further discussion revealed that each member feared being attacked, belittled, and hurt by the others and losing "face" in the eyes of the therapist. They viewed the therapist as an omnipotent judge with themselves as the accused.

Clients often fear that the therapist may destroy whatever delicate, fragile mechanism they have established for getting along. They may imbue the therapist with magical abilities to probe into what they say and reveal their hidden thoughts and feelings.

CLIENT EXPECTANCIES

Investigations have supported the contention that the client's expectancies of a successful outcome of psychotherapy relate to observed improvement (Goldstein, 1962). The exact nature of the relationship is unclear, but experimental evidence points to a curvilinear relationship. This means that people with moderate expectancies may improve more than people with extremely high or low expectancies. It is important to assess what the client's notions of psychotherapy are. Clients often hold unique theories regarding mental health and psychotherapy. For example, they may subscribe to a particular model of the therapeutic process:

1. *Adjustment model.* They expect psychotherapy to help them accept their feelings, problems, and limitations.
2. *Personality model.* They expect psychotherapy to remold their personalities into a new profile.
3. *Medical model.* They expect treatment to be like medical treatment, that is, they will be told by the expert what to do and will experience rapid gains with little involvement. Psychotherapy will be like swallowing a pill.

4. *Witchcraft model.* They expect psychotherapy to exorcise evil thoughts, feelings, and actions and to replace them with good ones.

5. *Moral model.* They expect the therapist to be a "good person" who will be able to teach them the right ways to act.

6. *Replacement model.* They expect the therapist to replace something missing in their lives (for example, friend, father, lover).

For treatment to proceed effectively, there may need to be a match between therapist and client expectations of the treatment process. It may be wise, for instance, to consider referring a client who seeks a particular kind of treatment (such as, psychoanalysis or primal scream therapy) that you are not able to offer. Before referring a client, however, the therapist should consider orienting the client to what he can usually expect in psychotherapy, providing a realistic assessment of its possibilities. In a family or work team seeking help, different members may adhere to different theories of effective therapeutic process. These differences need to be articulated before a course of intervention is designed.

THERAPIST EXPECTANCIES

Patient expectations *and* therapist expectations must be considered in order to establish a useful working relationship. It has been demonstrated that the dropout rate of non-YAVIS (YAVIS = *y*oung, *a*ttractive, *v*erbal, *i*ntelligent, and *s*uccessful) clients is considerably higher than that of YAVIS clients (Goldstein, 1971). The higher dropout rate of non-YAVIS clients may be traced, in part, to their failure to meet therapist expectations of what "good clients" should be. Non-YAVIS individuals may expect the therapist to demonstrate an authoritarian attitude, to provide direct advice, and to engage actively in intervention. If this runs counter to the therapist's theoretical principles, mutual dissatisfaction results. Similarly, therapist expectations that the client will be verbal and introspective, "open and honest" may actually run counter to the client's cultural norms and learning history.

> *Example:*   Pima Indians tend to show respect by trying to make themselves small, by not maintaining eye contact, and by not speaking very much. This behavior may be interpreted by the therapist as sullen, withdrawn, or hostile behavior.

Therapists often hold the expectation that highly motivated clients will perform better in treatment. They make more favorable predictions for such patients. Such clients are often better liked by therapists. Since patient-therapist attraction may be a salient ingredient in psychotherapy outcome, it is advisable that the therapist explicitly acknowledge and explore his own expectations. The therapist's biases or stereotypes may result in a self-fulfilling prophecy. For example, by expecting individuals diagnosed as "psychotic" to prove especially recalcitrant to treatment, therapists may tolerate greater deviations from appropriate behavior (for example, may allow "crazy" talk to continue uncommented upon). The therapist may feel discouraged and unmotivated to intervene with "psychotic patients" because he expects them to be "fragile" or presumes a poor prognosis. The client's failure to improve may then convince the therapist that his initial prediction was an accurate insight. He may pat himself on the back rather than attempt a modification of the treatment program.

The therapist may be expecting the client to have skills prerequisite to engaging in "therapeutic interaction." For example, children need to *learn* how to monitor their own behavior, see its consequences, and observe causal connections between events. If the therapist assumes that the child can naturally do these things, he may interpret incorrectly that the child is *not* a "good patient." In fact, Redl's *life -space interview* often has the effect of teaching children these "good patient" skills (see Section H).

We refer the reader to Goldstein (1962) who described a fascinating collection of studies directed at manipulating patient-therapist attraction through structuring expectations.

INDUCING EXPECTANCIES REGARDING TREATMENT

Some therapists provide an outline of what clients can expect from treatment. Fitts' (1965) *The Experience of Psychotherapy* is designed precisely to describe what the experience of psychotherapy is like for many clients and therapists. Cognitive organizers can be effective in facilitating learning in therapy. Role induction interviews have been used to advantage to acquaint the client with what he can expect from treatment.

Kelly (1955) often used a procedure he called *fixed-role therapy* for the initial weeks of treatment with his clients. This procedure involved writing a characterization of another person (different from the client's characterization of himself) and having the client role play that person in his daily life for two weeks. (The new characterization was constructed by Kelly from a self-characterization written by the client.) When fixed-role therapy is effective, the client will report that the new role model, which at first seemed impossible to enact, no longer seems very different from himself. The objective of fixed-role therapy is partly to show the client that some change is possible, that there is, in fact, another way of acting and viewing the world.

Lazarus (1968) hypothesized that setting up a graded structure with a succession of definite therapeutic stages through which a client can advance may facilitate therapeutic outcome. For example, with clients undergoing systematic desensitization treatment, one group was told that they would proceed from an elementary to an intermediate and finally to an advanced level. A second group was told only that it was helpful to master several relaxation sequences. Clients who

were given the graded structure tended to practice the exercises more conscientious-
ly and to receive greater benefits.

Simply reassuring the client that other individuals with similar difficulties have
been successfully treated will sometimes induce a positive and helpful expectation
about treatment.

*We suggest that the flow chart of this book be used as a mechanism to
structure the therapeutic process for the client.* The client will be told initially that
the first several sessions are designed only to understand the client's problems. The
first job then, the client is told, is not to change anything but simply to arrive at an
understanding of the dimensions and scope of these problems. The second job will
be to summarize these problems and to reach an agreement on what problems to
work on and how to work on them. This will be the contract. The client is told that
an agreement is usually reached but that sometimes therapists and clients agree not
to continue or to refer the client elsewhere at the contract stage. Only then, the
client is told, will structured initial change efforts begin. We have found that these
instructions relax the client and give the therapist a marker against which to gauge
progress. The client does not expect a "miracle cure" in the first two sessions and
neither does the therapist.

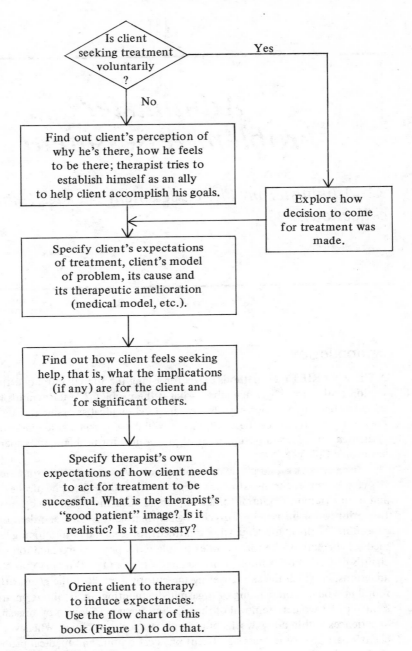

Figure 2.1. Flow chart of Section B.

III

Administer
Problem Assessment

C. Administer problem assessment package (initial data collection).

INTRODUCTION

A WIDE VARIETY of methods exists for asking the fundamental question of this section of the flow chart, namely, "What is the problem?" McReynolds (1970) edited two volumes reviewing advances in psychological assessment. This section does not plan to replace these volumes; it will provide some guidelines to the assessment process and outline a set of procedures for problem assessment which have some utility.

In many cases, and particularly for clients who complain of somatic difficulties (for example, chronic stomach pains, severe and frequent headaches, dizziness and motor tremors), referral for a complete medical and/or neurological examination prior to the initiation of psychological treatment is good standard operating procedure. With clients requesting treatment for sexual dysfunctioning, a complete medical checkup is essential in order to rule out a physical explanation of the client's distress. For example, Hartman and Fithian (1972) report that clitoral adhesions, in which the skin covering the clitoris is stuck to the glans, often are found in women complaining of orgasmic dysfunctioning. In about one-third of a sample of 83 women, removal of these adhesions was followed by orgasmic experiences within a few weeks of a simple surgical procedure. Whenever the client's past history reflects significant physical trauma and medical problems, the clinician should retrieve prior medical records (with the client's written consent). At times, especially with clients having a history of epilepsy or recent memory loss, neurological testing (including psychological tests, physical examinations, and electroencephalograms) may be helpful.

Sometimes inexperienced therapists are intent on "pinning" a label on the client. They think that once they know what to call him, for example, hysterical, obsessive, paranoid, they will know how to treat him. Too often, the multitude of questions asked to establish a diagnosis fail to establish any meaningful guidelines for change. We are suggesting that a really productive assessment leads naturally to intervention strategies. *A good assessment should suggest hypotheses for intervention* and not merely result in categorization or labeling. That is the guiding principle for this section.

WHAT WE WILL MEAN BY "PERFORMANCE"

We will use the word "performance" as a general term, not limited to motor skill. Performance will refer to the general functioning of the individual in cognitive, affective, interpersonal, and other behavioral areas.

We will talk about a "performance discrepancy." By this we mean that the client is performing in a way that either he or others (or both) feel needs to be changed. Often when a client requests help, he is affectively distressed. He may feel depressed, anxious, frightened, bored, angry, apathetic, hopeless, or inadequate. In any case his report of his feelings summarizes a life style that he would somehow like to change. The term performance discrepancy will also refer to these discrepancies between the client's perception of his current functioning and his expectations of how he would like to function.

SYMPTOMS, SYMPTOMS, SYMPTOMS

An operating assumption that we have found helpful in thinking of psychopathology from the point of view of planning interventions is to act as if symptoms were unimportant in themselves except as flags marking a need for intervention. Here is that assumption spelled out: We all have problems in living. For example, we may begin a semester refreshed from a vacation, excited about new courses and hopeful. During the semester we each experience thousands of problems and crises. We go through uncomfortable or painful social situations. We do things that impede our progress toward our goals. Things happen to us that we do not like.

Most of us, however, have ways of dealing with these problematic events. We can change our environment. For example, we may say, "Well, no sense in seeing *that* fellow too often in the future." Taking a vacation is a common method for temporarily changing our environment. Or we can change how we act. For example, a graduate student had a lot of trouble getting organized. He kept procrastinating, losing things, and forgetting things. So he went to a friend who was very organized and said, "Teach me how you do it." She did. He learned how to make "do lists" of what he had to do each day. At first he lost the lists. Then he followed them at great effort although the new behavior seemed artificial and phony. After a while the behavior was part of his repertoire and people started saying, "You're such an organized person. How do you do it?" "Just a natural talent," he would say.

We change our environment or our behavior to deal with problematic situations. We also change our cognition, or what we tell ourselves about events. When we are hired for a new job we can tell ourselves, "I'd better be on my best behavior. They're watching every move I make. I'm on probation, in a sense. I'm not really accepted yet." Or we can say, "They hired *me,* after all, not other applicants for the job. They must like *me,* so it makes sense for me to be as much myself as I can. Then if they don't like that at least I will not have been phony." Telling yourself the latter may make more sense because it is likely to lead to a more relaxed day-to-day existence.

So ordinarily we change our environment, our behavior, and what we tell ourselves. We *monitor ourselves,* our reactions to things and modify our lives to get what we want from our environment. In short, *we have operants,* or ways of operating on our world to get the reinforcements we want.

Symptoms then, are viewed as the person's struggle to get operants. Some operants do not work very well, come to the attention of public society, and are often labeled as "symptoms" of an underlying illness. The symptoms represent a wide spectrum of behaviors, and we are not much interested in why a particular symptom was chosen over another. This point is illustrated by the autobiographical writings of a psychotic woman, Lara Jefferson (1948). She wrote,

> We cannot cope with life as we find it, nor can we escape it or adjust ourselves to it. So we are given the power to create some sort of world we can deal with. The worlds created are as varied as there are minds to create them. Each one is strictly private and cannot be shared by another. (p. 18)

We feel that for too long the efforts of psychologists and psychiatrists have focused on the symptom itself and not on what the symptom tries to accomplish for the client. The client will be reluctant to give up the symptom unless he has an alternative, and he needs to learn an alternative way of having an effect upon, of operating on, his environment. To many clients, change offered seems like "out of the frying pan and into the fire." This is part of many clients' resistance to behavior change.

THE FOUR QUESTIONS OF PSYCHOTHERAPY

If the client has been referred for assessment, he may be there because he is not functioning the way *others* expect him to function. In this case the client may or may not share the expectations of others. Let us summarize this discussion by suggesting that it relates to the first question in assessment.

1. Why Is This Person Here?

If a case has been referred for assessment, the reason the client is there can usually be conceptualized in terms of *performance discrepancy.* There are two forms this can take. Either (a) the person is not performing the way he expects to perform, or, (b) the person is not performing the way others expect him to perform.

Do others report a discrepancy in performance they wish reduced to zero?

	Yes	No
Does client report a discrepancy in his performance he wishes reduced to zero? **Yes**		
No		

In the first case the client is likely to seek help because he is not as happy as he thinks he could be. In the second case the person is either not functioning the way other people like him to function—his performance may be compared to some *norm* of behavior (he may be a third grader functioning like a first grader, for example)—or he may not be functioning the way someone feels he ideally can function. His functioning is then being compared to some *criterion.* This may be due to a vague expectation others have of his "potential." If so, remember that expectations are in the head of the expector, and the problem is likely to be an interactional problem. The client may be unconcerned about his performance. Again, you may obtain valuable information by studying the labeling process. The label may be based on a norm-referenced or a criterion-referenced comparison. The comparison that has produced the discrepancy may also be tied to the client's past performance; for example, the client's performance may be inconsistent—at times surprisingly higher than his usual performance. A guiding principle in assessment is: *Remember that the client is doing the best he can do under the circumstances and yet he is still in a predicament. His characteristic ways of behaving, his characteristic ways of thinking, his problem solving skills (which generate new ways of behaving and thinking) are all not enough. He is stuck, and it's your job in this section of the flow chart to understand how he gets stuck, and why he stays stuck.* See Figure 3.1 for a summary of our progress in the flow chart before moving to the second question.

2. What Are the Objectives With This Case?

If a performance discrepancy has been demonstrated, then the objective may be to eventually reduce the discrepancy to zero. There are, of course, philosophical considerations in setting objectives which we shall not discuss here.

3. How Are the Objectives to Be Accomplished?

In the final box on the flow chart (Fig. 3.1) it is likely that you would begin thinking of the problem (and interventions) along the following lines.

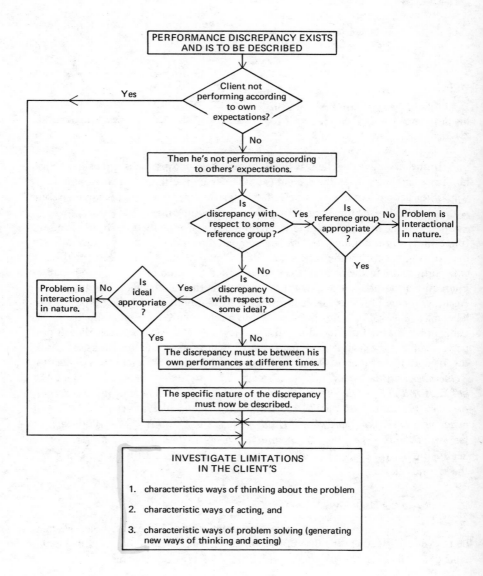

Figure 3.1. Flow chart of problem assessment.

1. The client is doing something he should not do, something disturbing to others (for example, parents, teachers, spouse, employer, police). Here the

treatment objective may be to decrease the frequency of the undesirable behavior either by modifying the contingencies of the behavior or the eliciting stimuli (or both). For intervention possibilities see Section E on response decrement.

2. The client is not doing something he should be doing. In this case there are one of two possibilities.

    a. He could do it if the payoffs were right or if the proper eliciting stimuli were present.

    b. Or he could not do it if his life depended on it.

In the former case you would want to restructure the contingencies or eliciting stimuli (or both) to increase the frequency of the desirable behavior. In the latter case above you would want to arrange for formal training for response acquisition (this includes teaching the client new problem-solving skills). For intervention possibilities see Section E on response increments and response acquisition.

3. The client organizes his experience in ways that do not permit him to predict events with much accuracy. We use the operating assumption here that the client *sorts* events into categories by responding to them in similar ways. For example, he may see all women as similar because they scare him, or all authority figures as similar because they anger him. The client acts as if he is telling himself something about his experiences which then becomes a new stimulus for action (such as avoidance of a class of stimuli). It may be important to know how the client sorts events. From the client's actions and verbal reports we infer a "cognitive structure." We feel that this way of conceptualizing the client's behavior will improve the therapist's ability to predict and influence behavior change. In a desensitization procedure, for example, this conceptualization suggests the hypothesis that transfer of training to extratherapy situations would be enhanced by having the client sort a deck of index cards describing situations in terms of the strength of his avoidance responses in these situations.

The intervention to change "cognitive structure" here might be to teach ways that are more effective (in the sense of improving the client's predictions) in sorting and discriminating events; the intervention might be to change what the client tells himself about his experience. See Section E for more specific suggestions on cognitive restructuring.

4. How will you know that these methods have accomplished the objectives? We will discuss the evaluation of progress toward therapeutic goals and the evaluation of interventions in Chapters 5, 15, and 16.

These are the general guides to the assessment of the problem for the purpose of generating hypotheses for intervention. We will now discuss specific assessment techniques and propose an assessment package.

THE ASSESSMENT PACKAGE

Although we will say very little about assessment using psychological tests, an orientation to testing may help. We feel that tests are often usefully considered to be a sampling of the client's behavior in certain situations, or a sampling of the client's report of his behavior. For example, an intelligence test samples certain areas of cognitive performance; an incomplete sentence blank samples some areas of the client's self-report. In general, we find it far more helpful to use an individualized assessment procedure to sample those behaviors and self-reports which relate to the reason that particular client is there seeking help. We do not, however, mean to imply that test batteries are not often valuable. They are useful if they help test differential diagnostic hypotheses that have different implications for intervention with the case.

In test construction any *test item* is considered to be an element in a *domain* of items which have some commonality. For example, in cognitive assessment, one domain of items may relate to numerical ability, another to spatial ability, and another domain to verbal ability. Let us consider what a test item is. Essentially a test item has three components:

1. *a situation* or a stimulus configuration,
2. *a task* or a response demand (such as multiple choice, matching, fill in the blank, talk to an interviewer, assemble a block design), and
3. *a criterion* or some way of assessing the competence of the response and some way of describing what a competent response would be.

In general we may administer a set of items or a test battery in the hope that we are appropriately sampling problem behavior (or behavior highly correlated to problem behavior). An alternative is to construct a domain of "items" for each client. Each item in the domain would have the same three components as a test item. It would have

1. a situation (stimulus configuration)
2. a task or response demand, and
3. a criterion or some way of assessing the competence of the response and some way of describing what a competent response would be (in that situation).

Discussing assessment using this analogy with test construction has powerful implications for intervention. It may serve to link assessment with psychotherapy. For example, one can teach an entire course using repeated testing interspersed with feedback, reinforcement, coaching, modeling, and behavior rehearsal. Suppose we wanted to teach you about Pavlovian conditioning and we could magically sample items from a large item domain to construct many parallel tests. The first test would be a pretest. We could discuss your answers and we could try to teach the concepts. Then you could take another test and again we could go over errors until eventually your performance reached an acceptable criterion level.

Psychotherapy could be conducted in the same way. Here are two examples.

Examples:

1. Mr. and Mrs. Mauter reported difficulty in making decisions together. A domain of problem situations was constructed which represented unresolved or poorly resolved issues between them. "Items" in this domain included sharing responsibility for the housework, spending time together, spending time separately, the family budget, taking vacations, and disciplining their five-year-old son. They ranked the issues in terms of the difficulty in reaching a decision. The housework was picked as the least difficult problem. The couple bought a cassette tape recorder and were asked by the therapists to tape a decision-making session about the housework. They dropped off the cassette a day before their session. In the session the cassette was played back to the couple. The therapists and each spouse could stop the tape at any time to discuss the communication. After some discussion, problems in reaching a decision were identified and some ground rules were set for the second family meeting. Again a cassette was made, and the second session was conducted in the same way. The process was repeated for each issue, although after the first three issues the couple moved to decisions quickly on their own.

2. A group of male "girl-shy" college students were seen in treatment by McFall (1970). A list of problem situations was drawn up by the group and coaching was used in role plays during group sessions. Homework was also assigned which involved problem situations such as talking to a girl on the telephone. Coeds were used in this therapy to help in some role plays and in giving feedback to the clients.

In these examples the therapist's job is a bit like that of a boxing coach. He waits for the bell between rounds, provides a bit of support, coaches the client ("Watch his left. He telegraphs that jab. Watch your footwork."), and then sends him back into the ring. The client's performance should improve on successive "rounds."

With this introduction, it will be helpful to briefly survey methods of assessment commonly utilized by therapists. There are several methods of assessment in current use.

Life History Assessment

The life history assessment uses questionnaires and open-ended or semistructured interviews to obtain a broad spectrum view of the client's life. The organizing dimension of this type of assessment is *development over time.* The client's early developmental history (starting with infancy and covering developmental milestones such as age of walking, talking, and toilet training), school experiences and adjustment, relationships with parents and peers, sexual awakenings, and such are all explored. Details of the client's current life, such as present living situation, work adjustment, companions, and his aspirations for the future are also investigated. A wide array of information may be gathered ranging from the client's sexual and occupational experiences to a thorough description of his present difficulties. Often, this approach appears more comprehensive than it actually is. A case history report is usually filled with some meaningless data, and the result is a *data overload* of both relevant and irrelevant information.

For individuals, the Wolpe and Lazarus (1966) Life History Questionnaire may suggest some areas worth exploring in the life history interview. For families, the Satir (1964) Family Life Chronology may prove useful. For couples with sexual problems, Masters and Johnson's (1970) History-Taking Outline may be employed. Remember that these are *guides*, not lockstep sets of questions to pursue. The interviewer should feel free to follow any area of importance that emerges and attempt to establish a natural flow of communication. He should be careful not to make value judgments or appear shocked, disgusted, or moralistic about anything the client says.

Psychological Tests

Psychological tests are frequently used for psychopathological diagnosis and intellectual assessment. The Wechsler Adult Intelligence Scale (WAIS), the Wechsler Intelligence Scale for Children (WISC), the Stanford Binet Intelligence Scale, and Bayley Infant Scale are the most commonly employed instruments for the assessment of cognitive functioning. Projective tests such as the Rorschach and the Thematic Apperception Test (TAT) are extensively used by dynamically oriented therapists. They are becoming less popular with behaviorally oriented therapists (McReynolds, 1970) because they have generally not shown up well in reliability and validity studies (Murstein, 1965). A useful discussion for generating hypotheses for psychological interpretation is given by Allison, Blatt, and Zimet (1968) and Rappaport (1968). A framework for conceptualizing psychological interpretation as hypotheses generating and testing is given by Levy (1963). Objective personality inventories which have been developed through the use of actuarial predictive methods (Meehl, 1954) such as the Minnesota Multiphasic Personality Inventory (MMPI) are finding an increased amount of use to evaluate therapeutic outcome (Lichstein, 1970). MMPI changes have been related to independent assessments of client change (Dahlstrom and Welsh, 1960; Schofield, 1966) and reliabilities are at acceptable levels. However, profile interpretations of the MMPI are questionable since factor-analytic studies show that the scales load on the same factor, an overall adjustment or adequacy-of-functioning dimension (Lichstein, 1970). Profile interpretations are best conceptualized as hypotheses requiring further testing. The Sixteen Personality Factor Questionnaire (16PF, Cattell and Eber, 1964) is a factor-analytically derived test which, although used infrequently by clinicians, overcomes some of the problems of the MMPI. The California Psychological Inventory (CPI, Gough, 1964) is an inventory like the MMPI but which does not stress pathology. Self-concept measures are frequently used in client-centered psychotherapy (Rogers and Dymond, 1954) to assess discrepancies between ideal and actual self-characterizations. The Q-sort (Block, 1961) is a commonly used assessment procedure in which the client sorts statements about himself on a dimension of how characteristic of him these statements are. Lichstein (1970) said of the Q-sort, "The economy of the Q-sort, its intimate relationship to client centered theory, and its demonstrated validity in outcome studies makes it the most useful of all self-concept measures." (p. 186)

There is a growing tendency on the part of behaviorally oriented therapists to use only those assessment procedures which offer some *prescriptive* as well as diagnostic guidelines. Sometimes standard assessment devices can be used with modified procedures of administration to generate hypotheses for intervention. An example of this is given below.

> *Example:*   An eight-year-old child was referred by the school for intellectual evaluation. He was given the WISC using a procedure which insured that he was paying attention. Attention was reinforced with candy delivered after each item. The child obtained a full-scale WISC IQ of 137 with this testing procedure. The school had thought the child might be retarded or brain-damaged. The implications of this testing were powerful in altering the school's expectations and in suggesting specific modifications of the child's educational program by reinforcing attending in the classroom.

Behavioral Assessment

Behavioral assessment includes an interview and *sometimes* involves:

1. *Personal construct assessment.* This includes the client's current perception of the problem, how he currently organizes his experiences, how he compares current events to past events, and his predictions of the future. Kelly (1955) developed systematic procedures for this type of assessment. (These are more commonly assessed using an interview. See the interview guide below.)

2. *In vivo assessment.* This usually involves the client's keeping a record of the frequency of a problem behavior, rating his subjective experience, or keeping a journal of relevant daily events. People other than the client can also be used for collecting base-line data. Self-monitoring of a behavior has been shown to have an effect on the behavior monitored (McFall, 1970; Gottman and McFall, 1972). Some behaviors that have been monitored to date include: rate of cigarette smoking, classroom talk, time on task, fighting, sexual intercourse, conversation time, deviant sexual arousal, study time, sleeping, severity of headache, mood, tension, anxiety, anger, hostility, depression, and fatigue (see Lichstein, 1970). Specially made record forms and graphs, wrist counters, and observations by significant others (such as spouses) have been found useful.

3. *Behavioral interviews.* They usually focus on the problem, its frequency and severity, the context(s) in which the problem occurs, the discriminative or

eliciting stimuli for the behavior, the consequences of the behavior, and the client's current limitations in solving his own problems. Often an "ABC" format is employed, that is, *a*ntecedents of the behavior, description of the *b*ehavior, and then its *c*onsequences are described.

4. *Performance by the client on simulated events.* Behavioral assessments have included observing the client in laboratory situations. For example, snake phobics may be asked to approach a snake and the distance of closest approach and subjective rating of fear are used to assess the severity of the phobia. Social situations involving parent and child may be used to observe family interactions and child behavior problems. The notion of a "simulator" as in space flights may be used to simulate a problem situation and assess the client's performance in that situation. For example, a husband and wife can be asked to make a decision and their styles of influencing each other can be observed. The extent to which talk time is shared, the extent to which subsequent comments logically follow preceding comments, the frequency of questions versus statements, the occurrence of summarizing statements, and the couple's and observers' subjective descriptions of the process of communication are examples of what can be assessed in a simulated situation.

We will now discuss how to conduct an initial interview, using these assessment procedures. Before meeting the client, it is wise to review the points discussed in Sections A and B of the flow chart. The client is approaching the initial contact with his therapist with as much trepidation and as many expectations as the therapist is approaching the client.

HOW TO CONDUCT AN INITIAL INTERVIEW

Many beginning interviewers frequently ask: What am I trying to get at in this meeting with the client? What should I generally go after? What is my general task?

Let us suggest two things you are after in an initial interview or series of initial interviews. Remember that a client usually comes to you because his characteristic patterns of living or ways of thinking about his world get him into some predicament. The center of the interview is the predicament itself and it is generally the interviewer's job to understand the predicament, that is, how it feels for the client to be in the spot he is in, what his typical ways are for solving the problems he faces, and why he is stuck. Within this context the interviewer works from the predicament outward, trying to understand three things:

1. the client's characteristic way of organizing his experience, making plans, and anticipating the future,
2. the client's characteristic pattern of living, and
3. the client's characteristic ways of problem solving (generating new ways to think and act).

Perhaps two metaphors would be helpful in this connection. One metaphor (Kelly, 1955) considers each man to be an amateur scientist who tries to organize his experience into a systematic framework that allows him to anticipate future events. A second metaphor (Goffman, 1959) views each man as an actor who plays certain roles in interacting with people. The client's cognitive system and his repertoire of behaviors may have limitations that relate to his current predicament.

Now, how do you go about "exploring" the client's characteristic ways of thinking and patterns of living? That's a good question. Well, you have two useful tools. First, one of your most useful tools is *your own ignorance.* You must recognize that you do not know what a client means when he says he is angry. Does it make him feel like he is about to explode, or like he is a bad person, or like he is losing control, or does he feel sad? This idea of the interviewer as basically ignorant may seem contrary to the idea of being empathic, but that is not necessarily so. Think of the interview as a trip through a client's world as he himself sees it. Remember that you are touring a foreign place, and like a good tourist you will need to ask the tour guide certain questions. If we push this analogy of the tour a bit further we come to the second useful tool. A tourist will try to ask questions that relate what he is learning about a new world to his own world. So your second tool is yourself. Your own feelings during the interview in interacting with the client are a valuable source of information. Do *you* feel at ease, or tense, or angry, or sad? Are there changes in your reactions at certain points in the interview? These feelings can be useful data about the client. You should observe the client's reactions during the interview, his anxiety, sadness, changes in his behavior, and problems in the dyadic communication.

For more discussion of the interview see Sullivan (1954), Kelly (1955), and Kanfer and Saslow (1969).

Structure of the Interview

The interview should follow a problem assessment format which is given below as a rough guide. We do not think this guide will fit all the cases you see, and we refer you to Kanfer and Saslow (1969) for another outline of a behavioral diagnostic procedure.

Situational analysis Unfortunately there is no systematic approach to the analysis of situations currently available. Perhaps the most useful metaphor we have found is a dramaturgical metaphor. In this metaphor every situation contains component parts.

1. The situational context which consists of
   a. the physical setting (the "stage" and "backdrop")
   b. the norms of that behavior setting, that is, the most frequent behaviors, those behaviors which are rewarded, those which are expected, and those which are punished in that setting

2. The task or objective in that situation (which is a function of the response demands of the situation)

3. The actors

4. The scripts of the actors

Examples:

1. Henry and Maude described one of their problems in the following situation. They were both on the way to a party with Henry's friends. Maude doesn't feel very comfortable with Henry's friends. They arrived at the party and Henry went off with the men while Maude was left to talk with the women. Maude felt bored by the "female" conversation and angry at Henry. On the way home in the car Maude told Henry she just would never go to another one of "these parties." Henry began to speed and this frightened Maude. Henry denied speeding, but said that he thought Maude was unreasonable.

2. Sharon Demerest is a singer who began to develop stage fright which made her voice quaver uncontrollably. She felt especially nervous if she thought that people from her church were in the audience. As she went out onto the stage she imagined these people coming up to her after her bad performance and telling her that it was "not too bad." She felt that the people in her church were taking advantage of her, making her sing at every church social as well as direct the choir.

3. Fritz Cohen answered an ad for "girl-shy" boys. One problem situation he described involved talking to girls at a party or mixer. He said, "It's always the same. The girls over there and the guys over here at first. Pretty soon they start pairing off. I guess I'm supposed to go up to a girl and say, 'What's your major?' But it's just no good. It never works. She says, 'Polish literature' and I don't know where to go from there. Usually I go back to my room and study."

In which specific contexts and behavioral settings does the problem occur? Which significant people are involved? Why these people and not others? Get a "play-by-play" description of the problem's occurrence in these situations. Get the *ABC*'s: What are the *a*ntecedents, what are the specific *b*ehaviors, what are the *c*onsequences? How frequently do these problems occur? Why is help sought now?

Assessment of the adequacy of the behavioral repertoire   Problematic behavior can be assessed in terms of competence by classifying it in terms of either *behavioral excess* (which entails an excess in either frequency, intensity, duration, or inappropriateness) or *behavioral deficit* (which entails deficit in terms of either frequency, intensity, appropriate form, or appropriateness). Behavioral deficit may refer to behaviors that exist to some degree but occur inadequately, or to the total absence of skill. The distinction is important since different interventions are suggested in the two cases (response increment or response acquisition).

Behavioral assets should also be assessed. What does the client do well? What are his skills? Or, if a client system is involved, what are the strengths of that system? In which set of role behaviors is competence observed? In which specific situations? In which situations is success highly or moderately probable? Often this assessment will provide an important starting point for structuring programmed intervention.

Controlling factors   What factors can "push" or "pull" the severity of the presenting problem? When is the problem stronger in severity, when less severe? In what situations is it more evident? Get descriptions of those situations in detail. In what situations is the problem less distressing? Why do these contrasts exist? What significant people are part of it? Why these people and not others? What sets the problem off? What can control it a bit? What interventions has the client tried on his own to handle the problem? What conditions seem to be maintaining the troublesome behavior? What are the *positively* reinforcing consequences of the problem behavior? What are the negatively reinforcing consequences? What does the client find reinforcing now? What is his past reinforcement history?

One semistructured way of approaching the question of controlling factors suggested by Lewin (1938) is called "force-field analysis." With the client, list the obstacles to solving the problem. What forces (people, situations) stand in the way of problem resolution? What resources exist that could help solve the problem? For example, a mother who feels trapped by her children may list going to school to complete an advanced degree as a resource but being unable to find or afford a baby-sitter, her husband's view of a wife's role, and her mother-in-law's influence on her husband as obstacles. There should be either the same or more obstacles as opposed to resources presently existing, which is presumably why the client is stuck. What does the client currently see as his alternatives for dealing with the problem? What does he perceive as the consequences of each alternative? What would happen and what would that mean to him? How does he think he can weaken or remove obstacles or strengthen or add resources for solving the problem?

How well does the client do in planning the *implementation* of an alternative solution to his problem? Does he have difficulty with the implementation phase?

Client's cognitive structuring about resistance to behavior change   It may be helpful to ask another series of questions regarding the secondary gains the "symptoms" provide for the client, that is, to focus on how the client might react to change efforts. What does the client think would happen if the problem were left alone, that is, what are the consequences of not finding a solution? What does the client think would happen if the problem were magically resolved? What would be different? What would the client do differently? What problems might be created by the change? Who would be made happiest by resolution of the problem? Who would be made least happy? Is this a problem? These questions are important especially when the client is presently functioning as part of a system, that is, family or marital. Often, a change in a spouse triggers off changes in the other spouse, or a change in one family member results in problems in other family members. By anticipating these problems, the therapist is better able to deal with them.

Past history   We feel that past history is relevant only to the extent that it is current; however, many therapists obtain a standard set of past history information. The client may have consulted other people in the past regarding his difficulties. He might have received extensive psychological or psychiatric testing. Requesting written permission to contact these previous agencies and individuals can often substantially reduce the therapist's work and prevent needless and expensive duplication of effort.

PEP TALK

It may take a number of interviews to investigate the areas listed above. You will often wish to supplement these interviews with additional quantitative data. Again, we are providing a *guide* for you to react to.

This may seem a bit overwhelming to you at this stage, but remember that the best teacher you will ever have on how to interview a client is the client himself. He is doing the best he can right now and that is not good enough. He is there with a story to tell, and you have got to help him tell it. Carl Rogers suggested the example of a man in a dungeon tapping out an S.O.S. on the brick wall with his tin cup. When the interviewer hears the client's story and the client knows that, it is like the prisoner hearing someone tap back, "I hear you."

QUANTIFYING BEHAVIORAL ASSESSMENTS

You will often wish to obtain other data to answer questions about the presenting problems. In Section A of the flow chart (Figure 1) we indicated that it is important to specify and study each setting in which complaints have arisen. Experience has tended to indicate that interventions may need to be planned separately for each setting. Behavioral assessment offers one way of directly assessing behavior in each specified setting.

Observation of the person or system can be made in real-life situations. Children are often observed either by home or classroom visits.

A useful method for *in vivo* assessment is to suggest that the client, family or system pretend or simulate the problem situation; role playing can be used to recreate the problem and assess the perceptions and feelings of people who were recently "in the situation."

When a family is seen for assessment it is sometimes useful for the therapists to invite themselves to dinner. Many beginning therapists at first feel uneasy about this but it usually makes sense to the families and a great deal of valuable information can be obtained just by visiting the family at home. With married couples, one of the authors has used cassette tape recorders placed in the home with the couple's consent operated by a voice key. The voice key turns the recorder on only when two voices are present. The data obtained by such *in vivo* procedures may be invaluable.

Example: A mother complained of hating her four-year-old son and was afraid she would hurt her child in a fit of rage. She, her husband, and the child were observed in combinations of play, instructing the child, and group projects; first the husband and child, then the wife and child, and then all three were observed. The wife appeared cold! She rarely smiled or touched the child but was able to set firm limits with the child. The husband touched and fondled the child and seemed warm. But he had difficulty setting limits. When all three were together, the child provoked his mother until she set limits with him. He promptly turned to the father for comfort and received it. This infuriated the mother, but she expressed her anger to the child instead of to her spouse.

Other persons in the client's environment may be involved with the client in data collecting and monitoring the client's behavior, its frequency, the situations eliciting the behavior, and its consequences. Self-monitoring procedures may also be used.

Example: Mrs. Jones tracked the frequency with which her child complied with instructions. She then plotted the percentage of times the child complied each day.

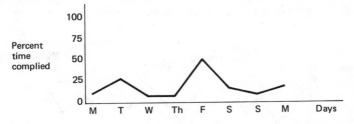

Something must have happened on Friday to have produced the peak and it would be worth finding out what it was.

A graph can be annotated with critical incidents which occurred that day which are presumed to be important to the behavior being observed.

Example: Mrs. Deer complained of the aggravating, attention-seeking behavior of her daughter Paula. Paula, she said, never gave her a moment's peace. Paula would throw temper tantrums, cry, nag, and whine. Mrs. Deer was asked to track positive and negative incidents using the form below. It became clear, after a week, that when Paula was quiet or played by herself, Mrs. Deer ignored her because, she said, "I'm so grateful to get a minute to myself; I don't want to do anything to set her off again." Eventually, Paula would seek attention and Mrs. Deer would yell at her. Paula's attention-seeking behavior occurred whenever Mrs. Deer had company or spoke at length on the telephone.

Date Time	Positive incident	What you did	Result	Date Time	Negative incident	What you did	Result

Mrs. Deer began reinforcing Paula's independent play and ignoring her pleas for attention at other times. The behavior problem gradually disappeared.

The client can rate the extent to which he experiences a presenting problem. He can graph his periodic ratings. He can also annotate this graph with critical incidents that seem to relate to the problem. Included in an annotated critical record, especially with adults, may be space for the client to indicate what he said and thought, both prior to and immediately following the critical incident.

Example: Mrs. Jones tried to improve her migrane headache problem. She tracked the severity of her headaches by rating them on a five-point scale.

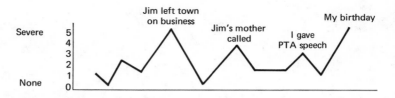

After seeing this chart, the therapist would want to explore with Mrs. Jones what it is about these situations that gives her a headache.

It is interesting to graph two or more variables over time to determine their relationship. One variable may vary concommitantly with another. Or one variable may be a lead indicator of another. One variable is a lead indicator of another if a change in the first variable is followed by a subsequent change in the second. For example, wholesale prices are a lead indicator of retail prices because if wholesale prices increase, retail prices will soon also increase.

Example: Mrs. Rogers complained that her three-year-old son Roy appeared depressed at home. His preschool teachers also complained to her of this behavior at school. Using a nine-point scale, the mother rated the extent of his depression as she saw it, and the teachers were asked to do the same.

Something at home appears to be related to depression at school since it appears from the graph that depression at home is a lead indicator for depression at school.

All of these assessment efforts must be considered *as a process of generating hypotheses for change efforts.* These hypotheses may be tested in psychotherapy. As more and more data are gathered, some hypotheses will be rejected and others will be supported.

In Section E of the flow chart we will return to a discussion of measurement for the purpose of evaluating change efforts. Evaluation should provide continuous feedback to the client and therapist for decision making during the course of therapy. Assessment, then, is not merely a process engaged in before therapy, but rather an integral part of psychotherapy itself.

SUMMARIZING THE ASSESSMENT: THE PSYCHOLOGICAL REPORT

The major reason for summarizing your assessment of the problem is so that you can discuss your findings with the client or clients during the contract phase of psychotherapy. What do you see as the major problems? What are the objectives you propose to establish with this case? How do you propose to accomplish these objectives?

What we recommend here is a serious departure from the traditional kind of psychological testing report. This report is designed specifically for the therapist and client as a basis for negotiating a contract.

We think you will always find it helpful to summarize your assessment in writing. In most clinical settings you will need to report your findings in writing for record-keeping purposes even if you continue with the case. Even if you do not continue with the case a written report is an instrument of social influence. It is designed to convince the reader of the validity of your inferences and intervention hypotheses.

Summarize your findings for each section of the book you have used in the case so far. You may describe:

1. Organizational systems of concern (see Fig. 1.1)
2. The decision to come for treatment, how client feels to be there, client and therapist expectancies (see Fig. 2.1)
3. Assessment package results
    a. performance discrepancies (see Fig. 3.1)
    b. interview results
        (1) situational analysis
        (2) assessment of behavioral repertoire
        (3) controlling factors
        (4) client's cognitive structuring about behavior change
    c. quantitative results of behavior assessment
        (1) base rates
        (2) critical incidents
        (3) concommitant variants
        (4) lead indicators

FURTHER READING ON THE INTERVIEW

Goffman, E. *The presentation of self in everyday life.* New York: Doubleday & Company, Inc., 1959.

Kanfer, F. H., and Saslow, G. Behavioral diagnosis. In Cyril M. Franks (Ed.) *Behavior therapy: Appraisal and status.* New York: McGraw-Hill, 1969.

Kelly, G. *The psychology of personal constructs, Volumes 1 and 2.* New York: W. W. Norton, 1955.

Masters, W., and Johnson, V. *Human sexual inadequacy.* Boston: Little, Brown and Co., 1970.

Satir, V. *Conjoint family therapy.* Palo Alto, Calif.: Science and Behavior Books, Inc., 1964.

Sullivan, H. S. *The psychiatric interview.* New York: W. W. Norton, Inc., 1954.

Wolpe, J., and Lazarus, A. A. *Behavior therapy techniques.* New York: Pergamon Press, 1966.

IV

Negotiate
Therapeutic Contract

D. Negotiate therapeutic contract: the alliance with the therapist to work on agreed-upon problems (agreed upon by all members of the "system"), including agreement about the manner in which treatment will be delivered.

JUST AS LOVE cannot be forced, neither can a productive therapeutic relationship. If client and therapist expectancies do not comfortably mesh, even after discussion, clarification, and exploration, it may be necessary to consider separation! The client might decide to seek a different therapist or type of therapy than the one you offer. A black client might decide he wants a black therapist; a female patient might opt for a female therapist; a Catholic client might want a therapist more sympathetic to her religious leanings. It may simply be the case that the therapist's personality or style of interacting does not inspire confidence or respect or trust in a particular client. Alternatively, the therapist may decide that he cannot do effective work with a particular client. Some therapists have difficulty working with alcoholic patients or seductive female patients or adolescents. It is not always simple for a therapist to refuse treatment to a client, especially when working for an institution that is paying his salary. Nevertheless, both the therapist and client are doing themselves a disservice if they disregard their feelings about each other and begin treatment with *major* reservations.

More often than not, client and therapist decide to work together and are ready to form an explicit treatment contract. This contract involves agreement on the goals, methods, and procedural rules of treatment.

There are no hard and fast rules about establishing such a therapeutic contract. Some therapists rely on verbal discussions while others actually use a written, signed contract setting down the conditions of treatment which is open to renegotiation throughout treatment. We recommend that a written, signed contract be used whenever possible.

IMPLICATIONS OF HAVING A CONTRACT

Goldstein, Heller, and Sechrest (1966) suggested that "giving patients prior information about the nature of psychotherapy, the theories underlying it, and techniques to be used will facilitate progress in psychotherapy." (p. 245) They go on to say that they find it "remarkable that psychotherapists have apparently been unwilling to impart to their patients more than a little of the process of psychotherapy." (p. 245) In effect, the client entering therapy is usually expected to buy a pig-in-a-poke. Good ethics suggest that the client has a right to know what he is getting himself into.

A contract will permit greater chance for making the therapeutic alliance operational. By having an unambiguous contract, indicating, if possible, the number of sessions reserved for treatment, subsequent disappointment resulting from unrealistic expectations or vague fantasies regarding the therapist (and therapy) may be averted.

A contract alerts the client to his role as an active participant rather than passive spectator. Negotiating a contract communicates to the client that his agreement and active involvement are essential to therapy. Hence, a contract will serve to discriminate the therapeutic relationship from the traditional doctor-patient relationship which often connotes "expert, authoritative doctor" and "ignorant, passive patient" suggested by Shakespeare in *Macbeth*:

> Macbeth: Canst thou not minister to a mind diseased, Pluck from the memory a rooted sorrow, Raze out the written troubles of the brain, and with some sweet oblivious antidote cleanse the stuffed bosom of that perilous stuff which weighs upon the heart?
> Doctor: Therein the patient must minister to himself.

Contracts may place a limit on the number of sessions. Often the result of a time limit is that more work is accomplished more quickly since both therapist and client understand and agree that treatment will not continue indefinitely. Both the therapist and client may feel more of an obligation to "do their homework."

The contract will serve to link specific therapeutic processes to concrete goals. Because of its ethical and practical value, we suggest that the contract stage of therapy be treated as far more than a trivial formality. You can expect the contract stage meetings with the client to be almost a formality in most cases. However, some clients will experience the summary of problems as upsetting and contract sessions with these clients are liable to be emotional sessions. It is important for the therapist to realize that summary feedback is often a difficult experience for anyone and to be sensitive to what the client may go through during these sessions. It is therefore important to ask the client what he is feeling, to discuss these feelings, and to reassure the client that this is a common experience.

THE PRESENTING SYMPTOM PHENOMENON

Often, the initial contract will lead to another contract which is more salient to the client. Sometimes the therapist feels that he is, at first, slaying dragons who sprout two heads for every one cut off. For example, the client may "test" the skill of the therapist by initially presenting a minor, but unworrisome, difficulty that he is perfectly capable of handling himself. Once reassured of the therapist's ability, the client may come out with the "real" problem—the one causing the greatest amount of pain or embarrassment or difficulty.

Example: After three sessions with an adolescent girl who had requested help with "examination anxiety," she suddenly blurted out that she thought she was a lesbian. She feared her own impulses toward women and felt guilt and shame when thinking about them. She was afraid to tell the therapist at first of her "secret problem" because she feared he would react with disgust and rejection.

Difficulties in therapy may also arise when not enough time has been devoted to problem assessment.

Example: Mr. and Mrs. Carlson came to the outpatient clinic because Mrs. Carlson had developed an intense fear of traveling. Although the therapist suspected that there were marital difficulties, the Carlsons refused to contract for such treatment. The therapist agreed, reluctantly, to treat Mrs. Carlson for her phobia of traveling and initiated systematic desensitization sessions. The treatment was quite rapid but the outcome was a surprise. The first thing Mrs. Carlson did upon terminating therapy was to pack her bags and leave her husband. Mr. Carlson was furious with the therapist and blamed him for the loss of his wife.

OPERATIONAL RULES, PROCEDURES, AND FEES

Part of the therapeutic contract involves the specification of treatment rules, including such issues as the need for regular appointments, calling before canceling, frequency of appointments, and payment of fees. Necessary clarifications of the therapist's operating procedures should be made here. For example, in family or marital therapy, the therapist may state that no session will be held if any member is absent. With sexual difficulties, the therapist may insist that the couple is the treatment unit rather than husband or wife alone. It is useful to state the issues regarding confidentiality. With adolescents, for instance, it may be agreed that all material is confidential but that if the therapist fears the client is going to hurt either himself or someone else, he may contact a parent (with the knowledge of the patient). Similarly, in family therapy, the therapist may refuse to listen to or keep secrets revealed by individual members which are communicated without the knowledge of the others (by confidential telephone calls, for example).

The fee issue should be explored early in treatment so that it does not become a major problem later on. Fees should be set in accordance with a client's ability to pay. Fees may be reduced but to increase them due to client wealth may be ethically debatable. Once set, the therapist has the right to expect payment. If payments are delayed, the issue should be brought up for discussion. Often, clients may use nonpayment of fees as a means of communicating their anger, disappointment, or dissatisfaction to a therapist and this becomes a major issue of therapy.

23-4/week 2

V

Set Objectives
of Initial Change Efforts

*E1.   Set objectives of initial change efforts; design
data-gathering procedures for continuous progress
assessment toward objectives.*

AT THIS POINT of the flow chart you have obtained: (1) a list of the problematic situations, (2) a play-by-play description of each problem situation, (3) a behavioral deficit and asset list in problematic and nonproblematic situations, and (4) have some idea of what the positive and negative implications of change would be for the client and the organizational systems in which the problem occurs.

You now have a fairly good answer to the first question of psychotherapy: Why is this person here? You should also be able to proceed to the second question, namely, what are the objectives of therapy with this case?

The question of objectives can be considered entirely apart from the question of how to accomplish these objectives. In fact, we feel that it is precisely the failure to separate goals and methods that has been particularly detrimental to the effort to evaluate psychotherapy. It is easy to become sold on a particular method of treatment as *the* answer for everything, particularly if the therapist has had a personally satisfying experience with that method (either as a client or as a therapist). Well, do not be easily sold. Use a method as a working hypothesis to be checked and tested. Use the same standards for yourself as you would apply to a drug company marketing a new drug. Demand evidence of effectiveness and modify your methods if they do not work, instead of changing client populations to fit your repertoire of treatment methods.

How can you obtain a list of goals from your problem assessment? Try asking yourself these questions:

1. What would these problem situations look like if I was a total absolute failure as a therapist, that is, if I made things worse?

2. What would these problem situations look like if I was a total absolute success?

3. What do you (and the client) predict would happen if things were left alone for ten years?

4. If you could play God, what would you alter to short-circuit the escalation of discomfort in each problematic situation? What would be the result?

Goals are *discrepancy statements* which compare current functioning to some *criterion* of competence or to some normative standard of competence in those situations.

SPECIFYING OBJECTIVES OF INITIAL CHANGE EFFORTS

An objective must contain four things:

1. Who?
2.   will do what?
3.   to what extent?
4. under what conditions?

Who?   The objective is stated in terms of what the client(s) will do, not in terms of what the therapist will do. This is crucial because it means, for example, making a therapeutic interpretation is *not* an adequate objective. An objective must be stated in terms of the client.

Will do what?   The emphasis is on doing something that can be observed in behavioral terms. For example, the objective that the client will "deal with the issue of loss" is inadequate. What behavior will be evidence that he has "dealt with" this issue? How can you tell? Many therapists will search for evidence after the fact instead of taking the trouble to specify ahead of time what will be acceptable and unacceptable as evidence. Unless this is done, the statement that the goal was attained is untestable, because it is not capable of being disproved.

To what extent?   A criterion level of performance is necessary. Otherwise, you will never know if the behavior exhibited was to anyone's satisfaction. A suitable criterion can always be generated by specifying that there will be a statistically significant difference between baseline and postintervention periods in the variable being monitored. This concept is easy to see if you assume for the moment that you can count the frequency of the desired behavior and it is your goal to significantly increase the frequency of that behavior.

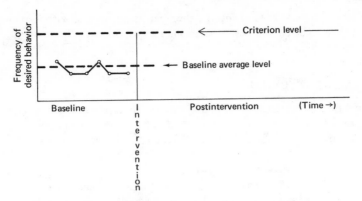

Figure 5.1.   Specifying a target criterion level.

In a later section, we will discuss how to arrive at a criterion level, and how to define what a significant increase is.

Under what conditions?   Assume that behavior has a high degree of situational specificity. It may be easier for a client to be assertive with his parents or spouse than with his boss or teacher. The nature of the first problematic situation to tackle in treatment will be determined by the step-size of the requisite behavior for the client. For example, in assertiveness training, the initial situation may involve using the telephone rather than a face-to-face encounter. It is important that the precise situations be specified.

> *Example*:   In discussing the issue of the housework chores, Henry and Maude will share the talk time. Henry will increase the frequency of expressing anger when he feels it; Henry will decrease the frequency of withdrawing from the conversation; Maude will decrease the frequency of whining, complaining, and blaming; Maude will increase the frequency of telling Henry directly how she feels. Each of them will use wrist counters to monitor talk time, clicking after each of their own statements.

PROXY VARIABLES

We introduce the concept of a "proxy variable" because often therapists have a great deal of difficulty specifying objectives. A "proxy" variable is a variable that in some sense traces the progress toward objectives without necessarily being as direct an assessment of progress as we would like. We want to give the therapist some methods of assessing progress toward goals which will inductively enable him to make the assessment more specific. For example, doctors use a patient's temperature as an overall index of health. It is a crude index, but nonetheless it has been found to be extremely useful. We hope that this section and the use of the "proxy variable package" will in fact teach the therapist how to specify, operationalize, and assess progress toward specific therapeutic objectives. With that end in mind, we digress to discuss how to operationalize *any* construct and design measurement procedures.

MEASUREMENT IN GENERAL

We feel that measurement of progress toward therapeutic objectives is so important that we are going to begin this section by teaching you how to operationalize and measure any particular construct you choose to measure. A common problem many people seem to have in designing measurement operations is that all methods of measuring a construct seem unsatisfactory. It seems to many people that "You just can't *really* measure ____." You fill in the blank with anything you want such as self-concept, dominance, happiness, mental health, or whatever.

Of course you can measure anything. However, measurement operations need to meet certain criteria. No operation or procedure for measurement meets all criteria perfectly. The extent to which it meets these criteria is the important question. For example, the Lone Ranger may administer a questionnaire in the Wild West to discriminate the good guys from the bad guys. Any measure of "goodness" is going to miss some good guys and get some bad guys. The extent to which the measurement operation is on target needs to be considered (especially before using those silver bullets).

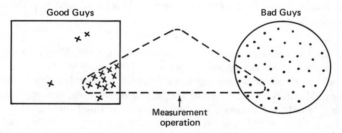

Figure 5.2. A criterion for evaluating a measurement procedure.

To get you unstuck from the "You can't do it" groove of measurement design we would like you to try the Chinese Menu Exercise.

Do the following exercise
before reading any further.
Go get a pencil or a pen.

CHINESE MENU EXERCISE

Select one from column A, one from column B, and one from column C below to complete the following sentence.

A	are more	B	than	C

A	B	C
Dogs	forgetful	crocodiles
Cars	curious	horses
Pigs	mysterious	armadillos
Mules	intelligent	badgers
Monkeys	creative	vultures
Giraffes	aggressive	pigs
Human (adults)	playful	cats
Human (children)	dominant	dogs
Kangaroos	sexy	mules
Lions		adult (humans)
Elephants		professors
Students		

Write your completed sentence below:

List three specific ways of assessing the truth or falsity of the sentence you generated. (Design measurement procedures and an experiment.)

OK. Perhaps that seemed a bit silly, but now try this problem and it will seem easier than it would have before.

Problem: Devise a way to measure a child's "self concept." Pretend you are seeing a child in therapy who appears to have a very low opinion of himself and his capabilities, and that his opinion is largely unfounded. Your supervisor says your therapeutic goal is to "raise his self concept." How will you measure progress toward this goal? Write your solution to this problem below.

Solution:

We will try to give you some feedback on your answer by telling you how we solved this problem with one of our cases.

Example: Self-Concept: In psychotherapy with a child who thought of himself as a "loser," the therapist constructed a "homemade" assessment procedure for operationalizing self-concept for this client. This procedure involved periodically listing situations the child was to encounter and asking the child to predict how well he would do. For example, here are seven situations that came up in the child's ratings.

Date: 12/3/72 Expect to do:	(1) Bad	(2) Average	(3) Good
1. Behave with the babysitter on Friday night _____	x		
2. Do well on math test on Wednesday _____		x	
3. Win at cards with my sister _____	x		
4. Win at hockey game _____		x	
5. Finish homework this weekend _____	x		
6. Not fight with sisters _____	x		
7. Not sass back mom _____	x		
TOTAL	5	4	=9
PERCENT OF MAXIUMUM = .9/21 = 43 percent			

His predictions were discussed in therapy. During the course of ten sessions a graph of his self-concept scores was plotted.

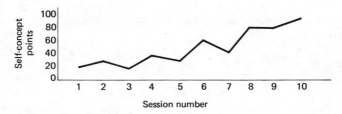

Scores were also analyzed separately for areas of self-concept involving parents, school, siblings, and peers.

We picked "self-concept" because it is an example of what many people have considered in the "unmeasurable" category. Part of the reason why things seem unmeasurable may be due to the "reification fallacy."

THE REIFICATION FALLACY AGAIN

In the practical problems of assessment facing the clinician, the first problem is to analyze performance discrepancies. In what situations are what behaviors not meeting what expectations? This seems to be a far cry from asking what quality is lacking in the client. In psychological measurement what has often happened is that an adjective modifying a noun has itself become a noun. We return to the concept of reification because it is important in measurement design. Specific intelligent behaviors in specific situations become "intelligence." Specific aggressive behaviors in specific situations become aggressiveness.

Changing the adjective to a noun assumes that there is a unitary dimension which a person now has a certain amount of. The specific behaviors and the specific situations have been dropped. The extent to which people's behaviors across situations are consistent is an empirical question. Mischel (1968) concluded that there is a great deal of situational specificity to behavior and that trait and state notions in psychology have largely failed to organize and predict human behavior. If this conclusion is warranted, then this part of reification (converting from an adjective to a noun) has low utility for measurement design.

One key toward designing measurement operations is to convert the noun back into an adjective. Then describe the situation in which the behavior occurs.

REMEMBER: Anything that occurs, occurs with some frequency and can therefore be *counted*.

Another valuable source of data for measuring a construct is archival data. *Archival data* are data gathered by a system as a normal part of its record keeping. For example, attendance, disciplinary incidents, grades, and achievement test scores are kept as a normal part of the functioning of a school. When treating a child in therapy who has a school problem, the therapist may wish to obtain archival data from the school before treatment begins, during treatment, and after treatment as an index of the impact of psychotherapy. Archival data often constitute valuable sources of inexpensive data which reflect the impact of treatment.

We will now discuss a concept of measurement design which may also deal with the "you can't *really* measure it" syndrome.

CONVERGENT OPERATIONS

The concept of *converging operational definitions* suggests that the most convincing evidence in assessment comes from using several different measurement operations *in conjunction*. The idea is that there is no one perfect measurement operation that is free of all criticism. Therefore it may make more sense to use several measurement operations in conjunction, each of which has different kinds of weaknesses when used alone. Webb *et al.* (1966) discussed this concept and recommended the use of unobtrusive measurement procedures as one category of measurement operations which needs to be considered. An unobtrusive or nonreactive measurement procedure is one which minimally affects what you are trying to assess. For example, if you wanted to assess the frequency of drinking in a dry state, an obtrusive way to do that is to go door-to-door and ask everyone how much they drink. An unobtrusive way is to count liquor bottles and beer cans in the city dump. An obtrusive way to assess the popularity of an exhibit at an art gallery is to ask people to rate exhibits in order of preference. An unobtrusive way might be to measure the amount of wear on linoleum tiles in front of the exhibit compared to wear elsewhere in the gallery. The idea is not that unobtrusive measures are best, just that they are not beset with precisely the same problems as other operations. Remember the point is that the most convincing measurement evidence comes from the convergence of several different measurement operations used in conjunction. This leads us to our discussion of the *proxy variable package.*

MEASUREMENT: PROXY VARIABLE PACKAGE

We are going to suggest five procedures for gathering data over time for the evaluation of psychotherapy. These are not necessarily the best methods. Physiological measures for assessing muscle tension may be superior to self-ratings and are becoming more portable, inexpensive, and practical tools for the psychotherapist. But until such instruments are in common use the question of measurement rests largely upon the development of inexpensive measurement operations with a fair degree of utility and validity. We want to offer some specific suggestions. However, we do not think that these suggestions should limit the therapist. In fact, the purpose of the Chinese Menu Exercise was to encourage the therapist to construct his own measurement devices.

Ratings Made by the Client

Ratings made by the client (and others) assessing the client's perception of the *extent* of or *severity* of a variable can be made periodically as a regular part of treatment. These ratings over time become a quantitative linguistic tool and take on a high degree of face validity. Ratings over time can be valuable if they are annotated by critical incidents that can serve to link fluctuations to specific kinds of situations.

Example: With migraine-headache patients, Budzynski, Stoyva, and Adler (1970) found a high degree of relationship within subjects between the subjects' ratings of severity of headache (on a five-point scale) and electro-myographic recordings of frontalis (forehead) muscle tension.

Grace and Graham (1952) reported that a common situation precipitating migraine headache onset was the individual's striving to meet a deadline, achieving an objective which involved potential success or failure.

These two results suggest that with migrane headache patients an annotated diary rating over time may be useful.

Ratings can be obtained simultaneously on a variety of salient dimensions and plotted over time.

Examples

1. Extent to which the patient feels he has choices as opposed to feeling trapped

1	2	3	4	5	6	7	8	9

Feel trapped   Neutral   Many alternatives are available

2. Extent to which patient feels he is appreciated

1	2	3	4	5	6	7	8	9

Not at all   Neutral   Very appreciated

3. Severity of depressions

1	2	3	4	5	6	7	8	9

Not at all   Thoughts of suicide

4. Severity of feelings of anger at work

1	2	3	4	5	6	7	8	9

Not at all   Furious

The poles of the dimensions can be arrived at with the client. The poles of the anger dimension, for example, for a particular client might be:

1	2	3	4	5	6	7	8	9
submissive				in control				ready to explode

and are thus confounded in his mind with an assertiveness dimension. Ratings should be made at least daily.

Frequency Counts by Monitoring (by Self and/or Others)

Data gathering by frequency counts and charting over time is commonly suggested by behavior therapists. The point about measurability again is that if an event occurs, it occurs with some frequency and can therefore be counted and graphed.

Although it is more common to count specific behaviors, it is also possible to count the occurrence of subjective events. For example, in the introduction we discussed the example of piloting a new measurement procedure which uses golf counters to count the occurrence of unpleasant and pleasant behavior exchanges with a married couple. Again a critical incident diary might be useful in defining more precisely what each spouse considers a negative or a positive exchange. This kind of frequency counting can have some validity. With two couples in treatment at the time of this writing, the difference between total daily negative exchanges was calculated. This variable was called "daily points earned." Couple 2 seemed to be in a state of more severe crisis at the beginning of treatment. They had been married for seven years and had each separately been in treatment for three of those years. They reported that they had not had sexual intercourse for eighteen months. They considered therapy "one last attempt before the lawyer." Couple 1 had been married for three years and their problems seemed less severe. The therapists also consider both couples to have made "significant progress" in therapy, although they say that Couple 1 is currently "in better shape" than Couple 2. The table below presents the average daily points for both couples for the first week of therapy and the current week (at the time of this writing). This table was computed after the above subjective impressions of the therapists were obtained. These data fit with the therapists' subjective impressions of these cases.

Average Daily Points Earned

	Couple #1		Couple #2	
	Then	*Now*	*Then*	*Now*
Earned by her	-.08	2.50	-1.75	.00
Earned by him	1.04	2.50	-1.85	.00

It is far more common to count and graph the occurrence of specific observable behaviors. However, during a problem assessment phase of treatment the monitoring of subjective events coupled with a critical incident diary may give the therapist an idea of which specific events are most salient for a particular client.

Critical Incidents

It is useful to use incidents the client considers important in his life, and to annotate other data collection procedures (ratings and frequency counts) with those critical incidents. This can be facilitated by having the patient keep a journal or daily log.

A common example of an annotated record over time is given by the Dow Jones Industrial Average (monthly averages plotted).

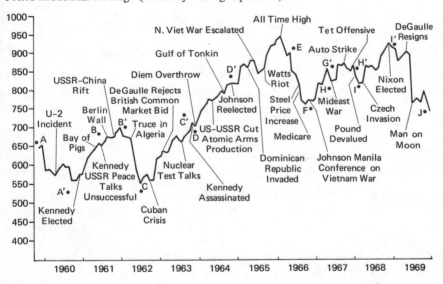

Figure 5.3. Annotated record of Dow Jones Industrial Average.

Such an annotated record can be used by the therapist to generate hypotheses about events which may control fluctuations in the patient's record.

Another interesting way to use critical incidents is to detail a play-by-play account of an incident that recurs in the client's life and is part of the problem. For example, the therapist can ask a married couple to write detailed accounts of arguments they have. There may be characteristics of the argument that suggest interventions for treatment.

Posttherapy Session Evaluation Sheet

Before the end of each session it may be useful for both the therapist and client (or client system), to fill out a postmeeting reaction (PMR) form, and perhaps compare responses. A PMR which has proven to give very useful feedback and is also quick to fill out is shown below. Critical incidents can be sorted into categories when collected over time, ratings can be plotted as charts, and these charts can be annotated with critical incidents.

Date: _____ Therapist(s): _____

Client Name(s): _____

POSTMEETING REACTION FORM

1. Please circle the number below that best reflects your feeling about the session:

    1   2   3   4   5   6   7   8   9
    Bad   Good

2. Briefly describe one positive and one negative critical incident that happened in the session that explains your rating.

(+ positive)

(- negative)

Simple 1 to 9 ratings become a language of their own over time. A client will come into a session saying "It was a 5 day, nothing special, nothing terrible," or leave a session saying, "Well, I'd give *that* session a 2." The therapist can model and encourage the use of the rating scale in this way and the use of critical incidents over time can provide some valuable feedback as to how to treat this particular client. A more extended form for assessing the client's reaction to both his own behavior and the therapist's behavior at the conclusion of each session may be found in Lazarus (1971).

Archival Data

Archival data were discussed earlier under the section on convergent operations in measurement. They often form a valuable source of information to evaluate the general progress of the patient over time. They are also an inexpensive index that trace the overall functioning of the patient.

The chart below is a brief summary of the measurement package we suggest for the inexpensive monitoring of psychotherapy.

Suggested Inexpensive

Proxy Variable Package

A. Obtain ratings made by client on a dimension and plot over time.	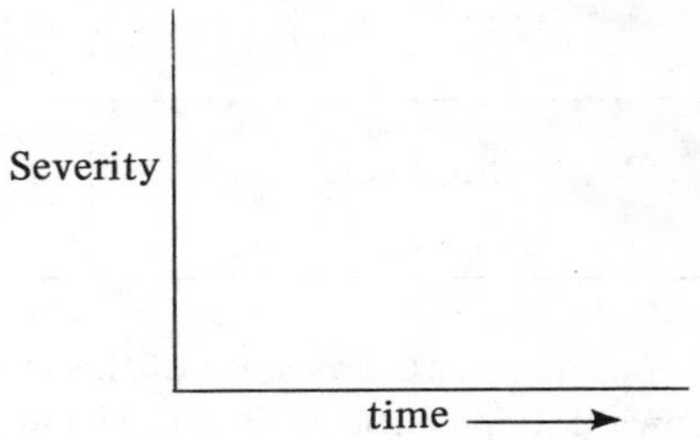 Severity time 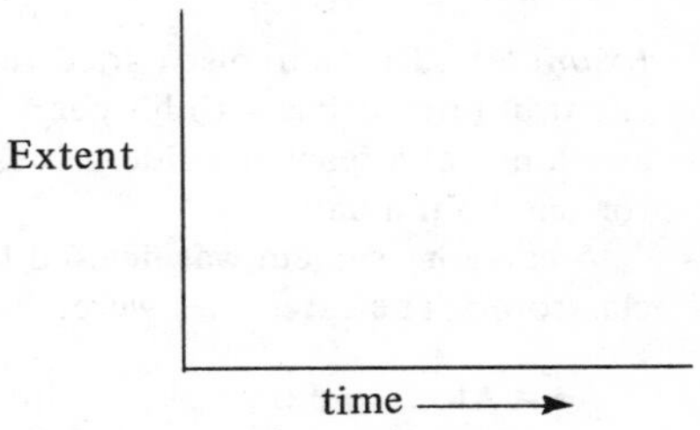 ⟶ Extent time ⟶
B. Count frequency of an event plot over time.	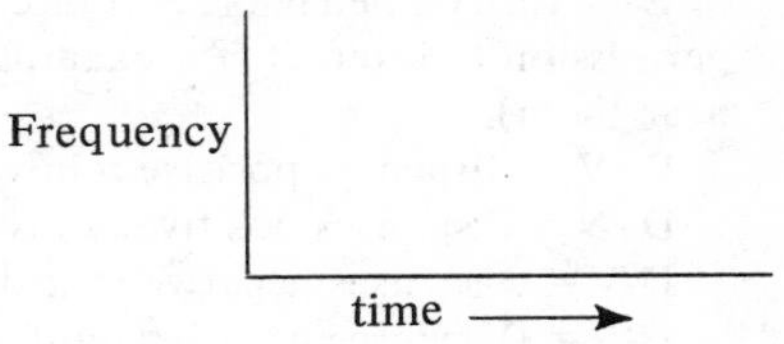 Frequency time ⟶
C. Critical incidents 1. Have client keep journal of extratherapy events along with ratings (severity, extent).	See Chapter 16 of book for example of a journal and its use with a rating scheme.

2. Obtain a play-by-play account of a current problematic situation.	
D. Posttherapy Evaluation sheets	See page 58.
E. Archival data	See page 58.

The essential message of this section is that the therapist can assess progress toward therapeutic goals if time and imagination are applied. Perhaps some examples would be interesting. The example below illustrates the use of behavior observation techniques in therapy with a social isolate.

Example: The therapist visited the classroom to observe the behavior of his client in interacting with his peers. He was subsequently able to obtain the assistance of a teacher's aide to observe systematically the client's behavior for one hour a day.

A category system was devised for observing the child's behavior in the classroom. The categories were:

A+ = Alone and on task; not interacting with other children or with the teacher, but listening to the teacher or attending to the task on hand.

A- = Along but not on task (for example, tuned out, day dreaming)

E = "Entry" behavior. Not interacting but seems to be requesting permission to interact (for example, watching other children and standing near them).

D+V = Dispenses positive reinforcer verbally to peer.

D+N = Dispenses positive reinforcer nonverbally to peer.

D-V = Dispenses negative reinforcer verbally to peer.

D-N = Dispenses negative reinforcer nonverbally to peer.

R+V = Receives positive reinforcer verbally from peer.

R+N = Receives positive reinforcer nonverbally from peer.

R-V = Receives negative reinforcer verbally from peer.

R-N = Receives negative reinforcer nonverbally from peer.

T+ = Receives positive reinforcement from teacher.

T- = Receives negative reinforcement from teacher.

Category E, required the most judgment on the observer's part. The following patterns were observed frequently.

Pattern 1:   A+, A+, A-, E, E, A-, A-, T-

Pattern 2:   A-, A-, E, E, E, E, D-V, D-N, R-N, T-

Pattern 1 was more frequent than Pattern 2. In Pattern 1 the child never goes beyond the entry stage of interacting, and calls the teacher's negative attention by having spent so much time withdrawn (A-). In Pattern 2, he does interact, but only by initiating negative interactions, which lead to his hitting, getting hit, and again receiving the teacher's negative attention.

The therapist then observed the interaction of other children in the classroom who seemed to be more popular. He found that they differed from his client in the amount of positive reinforcement they dispersed, but *not* in the amount of negative reinforcement they dispersed. He asked these other children to role play ("pretend") getting into a group of other children. From these role plays, he designed an intervention program to teach his client how to do simple things like greeting, asking a question, saying something nice ("That's a neat model car. Can I see it?"), giving information, and inviting other children to join him in an activity. These were essentially the techniques used by nonisolates in that classroom in "entry situations."

At the end of the intervention program the isolate had made a friend (and there is a world of difference between *no* friends and just one pal). He was also interacting with other children more, and receiving more positive reinforcement from both his peers and the teacher.

Throughout the training program the therapist was able to use the classroom observation data to assess the effectiveness of each subskill he was teaching his client.

Before we begin a discussion of how to engineer initial change efforts, a word must be said about what specific criteria any measurement operation must meet. If one problem has been the unwillingness of therapists to operationalize and individualize therapy goals, another problem has been the proliferation of instruments which purport to be all things for all clients.

SPECIFIC CRITERIA

Reliability

A measurement operation is said to be reliable to the extent that it gives similar readings under similar conditions. For example, if I am manufacturing thermometers, I may want to test samples of my thermometers. If I have an oven at a fairly constant temperature, I can specify that the temperature readings of my thermometer should come within a certain fraction of a degree of the oven temperature. I could also test how reliable a thermometer is by measuring that oven twice "under the same conditions" and seeing how close the readings are.

Now here is a problem with the concept of reliability for the behavioral sciences: What does "under the same conditions" mean in the behavioral sciences? For example, if I measure a child's intelligence with a new test when he is seven years old and get 103, and then measure it again a year later and get 120, do I conclude that the measurement procedure is unreliable or that his intelligence has increased?

In test construction there are several ways to assess reliability:

1. *Stability* (test-retest): the correlation between two successive measurements with the same test or inventory (must assume the two occasions of testing are "similar conditions").

2. *Alternate form:* two forms can be constructed by randomly sampling from a domain of items and a correlation computed between "equivalent" forms (random sampling from a domain, however, is not the usual procedure).

3. *Split-half:* a procedure used in place of alternate forms by dividing the items on one form in half, hopefully into "equivalent" forms.

There is another problem with the concept of reliability. In the thermometer example, if the mercury is stuck, I will *always* get the same reading, so the thermometer will be very reliable. But a person with fever, a normal person, and a dead person will all register the same reading. This necessitates introducing a new concept.

Validity

A measurement operation is said to be valid to the extent that it measures what it's supposed to measure. How do you determine if a procedure measures what it is supposed to? If a patient in a hospital has a temperature of 98.6 and his forehead is hot to the touch and he is acting delerious, you would probably want to use a second thermometer to check the first one. So, by "measuring what it is supposed to measure" we mean that the measurement operation correlates highly with other ways of measuring what appears to be (generally) the same thing. In test construction there are several ways to assess validity:

1. *Content validity* assesses how well the items on this test adequately sample the particular situations under consideration.

2. *Criterion-reference validity* assesses how well this individual's performance on this test predicts his performance in future related situations (for example, does the SAT predict grades in college?)

3. *Construct validity* assesses how well the test makes accurate predictions derived from some theory or conceptual model about the construct which the test purports to measure. This is vague. A good example is given by the notion of face validity. Suppose you show that 92 percent of all high school seniors in a city cannot read election ballots with comprehension. The set of items written directly from election ballots is "valid on its face," or obviously assesses what it claims to assess.

Yet another criterion needs to be invoked.

Utility

What is the cost of the information in relation to the benefit the information adds to making a decision? Is there a cheaper way to get the same information? If I have an 800-item test which is fairly accurate in predicting a person's height, that is a test of low utility because I can usually find out his height much more easily.

That's an absurd illustration, but Mischel (1968) raised the question of the utility of all "indirect" methods of personality assessment. It turns out that the best predictor of future performance is usually past performance in a similar situation. The next best predictor is usually obtained by asking the person to predict his own future performance. See the *Journal of Consulting and Clinical Psychology,* June 1972, for a discussion of the direct versus indirect assessment issue. A United States Air Force study was designed to predict the adjustment of airmen to duty in Alaska. Among a host of personality and demographic variables was the item that predicted best—"Do you like cold weather?" (Chester Harris, personal communication). The best predictor of verbal ability in an inventory was an item asking the subject to predict where he would score in relation to his peers: it correlated 0.68, the highest correlation in the matrix (Ann Cleary, personal communication). The point is that cheap, direct ways of assessment may have utility.

Remember that the use of test construction methods and terminology has general application to the design of measurement operations in psychotherapy. Test items are situations with stimuli that require the subject to respond. Test items also contain some way of assessing the competence of a response. From a domain of items we construct a test. Similarly, if we want to monitor the client's progress toward goals we can list situations which are problematic for the client and define competence in these situations. We can then assess the subject's performance over time on samples of situations from the domain and so assess the development of competence over time.

Ideally, we would like to use measurement procedures that make sense, that is, have high face validity and do not take much time or effort. For example, it might be interesting to do content analysis of audiotapes of therapy sessions to find out how many optimistic and pessimistic statements the client is making about the future. It might be interesting to track the percentage of optimistic statements during therapy sessions and predict an increase over time. Mowrer *et al.* (1953) did just this, but such a procedure is an unlikely tool for most practicing therapists without budgets for research.

We would, therefore, like to find *cheap* measures that tell us what we want to know about the progress of psychotherapy. The measurement package we have proposed is an attempt to meet these criteria [see also Mowrer *et al.,* 1953, and their use of the Discomfort Relief Quotient (DRQ)].

VI

*Engineer
Initial Change Efforts*

E2. Engineer initial change efforts.

THERE ARE AS MANY ways to do therapy as there are therapists doing it. Although theories, techniques, and practictioners differ, all change efforts involve focusing, at some point, on the client's view of his world (his cognition), what he is doing in his world (his behavior), and the world in which he operates (his psychological and physical "life space" or environment). While emphasis varies both between therapists and over the course of therapy, each of these variables must, inescapably, receive some attention. This chapter will list techniques for dealing with a client's difficulties by: (1) clarifying and changing his view of the world (his cognition): (2) changing his responses to the world (his behavior); and (3) changing the world in which he lives (his environment).

How are you to decide what problem to focus on first as the initial target of your change efforts? We suggest that, above all, this decision be made, to the greatest extent possible, with the full participation of the client in the decision-making process. Be responsive to what the client requests. If he wants help in accepting his homosexuality, do not set up a treatment program designed to help him find rewards in heterosexuality. Respect for your client implies respect for his diagnosis of his needs and wishes. Your job is to treat where the client hurts—not to prescribe the hurts he should have.

We refer the reader to an excellent paper by Haley (1969) called "The Art of Being a Failure as a Therapist" in which he suggested how the therapist can increase his chances to fail. Here is a summary of Haley's points plus some of our own on the subject. Chances for failure can be increased by:

1. Insisting that the problem the client brings to therapy is merely a "symptom" of another problem. The therapist can direct the conversation elsewhere every time the client returns to his "symptom" and mistakenly suggest that something deeper is really bothering him.

2. Refusing to set up a treatment program which focuses on the presenting problem the client thinks he is paying his money to recover from. (In this way the therapist can also avoid learning those specific skills he would need to help people with their problems.)

3. Telling the client that if the presenting problem is solved something far worse will develop. This will also encourage clients to develop a fear of recovery.

4. Confusing diagnosis with treatment and formulating the diagnosis in such a way that it cannot lead to any therapeutic interventions.

5. Placing the emphasis on a single method of treatment for all problems and condemning clients who do not profit from this method as "unsuitable candidates for therapy" or as untreatable.

6. Having an ambiguous or untestable theory of what the therapist can do to bring about change. Then, the therapist need only vaguely refer to the "process of the hour" and accept reassurance from colleagues that things are going about as well as can be expected. Haley adds:

> Should student therapists who are not yet properly trained insist upon some instructions about how to cause change, and if a frown about their unresolved problems does not quiet them, it might be necessary to offer some sort of ambiguous or general idea which is untestable. One can say, for example, that the therapeutic job is to bring the unconscious into consciousness. In this way, the therapy task is defined as transforming a hypothetical entity into another hypothetical entity and so there is no possibility that precision in therapeutic technique might develop. Part of this approach requires helping the patient "see" things about himself, particularly in relation to past traumas, and this involves no risk of change. (p. 693)

7. Insisting that only years of therapy will bring about "real" change.

8. Insisting that people are fragile and are likely to suffer "psychotic breaks" if the "underlying pathology" is not "dealt with."

9. Focusing on the client's past.

10. Ignoring the real world in which the clients live and emphasizing their infancy, inner dynamics, and fantasy life.

11. Avoiding the poor who will insist upon results and will not be distracted by insightful conversations. Only work with YAVIS (young, attractive, verbal, intelligent, and successful) patients.

12. Refusing to define the goals of the therapy except in vague terms so that no one can ever know if the goal has been achieved except by asking for the therapist's opinion.

13. Avoiding evaluation of the results of therapy. It is essential to make all decisions in therapy on an intuitive basis and to avoid following up clients in any systematic manner.

Finally, Haley suggested that the therapist can be assured of failure by following the "Five B's":

> Be Passive
> Be Inactive
> Be Reflective
> Be Silent
> Beware

BEHAVIORISTIC AND HUMANISTIC APPROACHES: THE FALSE DICHOTOMY

Behavioral approaches have sometimes been criticized as inhuman, manipulative, cold, or callous.

As London (1964) pointed out, therapy is, by definition, a moral enterprise. Implicit in all therapeutic decisions is some idea of how people should behave (for example, sexually liberated versus sexually inhibited), how they should feel (for example, guilty, shameful, anxious versus relaxed, tolerant of self, gratified in love and work), and what they should want. Whether the therapist nods sagaciously, remains silent, or actively berates the client, he communicates approval or disapproval of the client's words which the client necessarily interprets. Rather than hide behind the smoke screen of impartiality and pure objectivity, let us state some of the moral and ethical stands we have taken in these chapters.

We have adopted an action- rather than insight-oriented position and, with it, have acknowledged that the therapist is primarily responsible for the course and outcome of therapy. We will speak of resistance, not as an attribute of the patient that impedes successful outcome, but rather as an indication that something might be amiss in the therapist's approach to and relationship with the patient. We will suggest the use of conditioning and counter-conditioning techniques to change behavior and will sanction the use of aversive procedures where they seem uniquely beneficial to solution of the client's difficulties.

Each of these judgments may be (and has been!) the subject of heated debate among practitioners of various theoretical orientations. Insight-oriented therapists allege, for instance, that the "actionist is sterile, superifical and mechanical . . . and fails to apprehend the great variety of human ways and ultimately sacrifices the meaning of any man's existence to a quest of comfort and adjustment, freeing him of a need to discover his self" (London, p. 137). Bettelheim (1967, p. 410) attacked operant procedures as coercive and dehumanizing processes which treat people as objects. He accused behaviorally oriented therapists of stripping away individuals' defenses, and reducing "autistic children . . . to the level of Pavlovian dogs." He stated: "To create conditioned responses in the patient deprives him just as effectively of the human freedom to make choices, as does the destruction of part of his brain." (p. 411)

To the charges advanced specifically against behavior therapy, we refer the reader to the excellent discussions of the rationale and ethics of this approach in Ullmann and Krasner (1965) and Bandura (1969). To quote Ullmann and Krasner briefly,

> traditional therapists' objection to behavior therapy in terms of the overt application of learning principles seems unwarranted when viewed in the light of their dogmatic application of a theory that overrides the patient's wishes, their actual procedures of indoctrination, and the loss of efficiency by haphazard use of the therapeutic situation. (p. 41)

We also wonder whether the judicious use of aversive conditioning procedures is not at times humane. It may be disturbing to us that our natural response inclinations are ineffective, but that is often the case. Our inclination with an autistic child banging his head may be to pick him up, hug him, and tell him he is loved. Indeed, that seems like the humane thing to do. But is it in fact? Lovaas *et al.* (1965) found that such responses by an adult would be followed by an *increase* in self-injurious behavior. In contrast, Tate and Baroff (1966) found that withdrawing body contact and the use of brief but intense electric shock led to the complete elimination of the self-mutilating behavior without its recurrence later.

The point is that being humane may mean *not* responding naturally, but thinking and engineering change in a methodical, scientific way. Another example may illustrate this point. In teaching speech to psychotic children, Hewett (1965) made use of a teaching booth. The teacher sits in one half of the booth and is separated by a shutter from the child. When the shutter is open the child is in eye contact with the teacher and his attention can be focused on the teacher's mouth for speech training; when the shutter is closed the child is in darkness which serves as an aversive stimulus that motivates the child to perform in order to produce light and human contact. Perhaps this sounds cruel. Yet the sheer difficulty of controlling the behavior and attention of the psychotic child in the initial stages of training and the beneficial results obtained by the application of this procedure would seem to justify its use.

The very words "behavior control" generate more heat than light in discussion. Acknowledging that a therapist is actively engaging in prediction and control of a client's behavior often is linked with the image of a satanic demon with Machiavellian intent and beset by delusions of grandeur and power. Yet even Rogers, the leader of the client-centered school of therapy that advocates nonjudgmental, permissive, and unconditionally positive attitudes has conceded that "in client-centered therapy, we are deeply engaged in the prediction and influencing of behavior, or even the control of behavior. As therapists, we instituted certain attitudinal conditions and the client has relatively little voice in the establishment of these conditions. We predict that if these conditions are instituted, certain behavioral consequences will ensue in the client." Krasner (1962) is even more explicit. He has referred to "The therapist as a social reinforcement machine" who, "programmed by prior training and experience, is devoted to using his behavior as a decisive factor in interpersonal situations with individuals requesting assistance. His goal is to influence his patient's behavior in the therapy situation so that certain changes may occur in the patient's total life situation."

The crucial issue becomes whether the therapist's power and skill in influencing others to relinquish maladaptive behavior and learn adaptive skills is used for his own advantage or that of his client. And we hasten to add that all therapists—of whatever orientation—see themselves as working on behalf of their clients. We have attempted to make explicit our belief that crucial therapeutic questions, whether it be the selection of a specific treatment goal or the decision to employ a particular therapeutic technique, be made with the understanding and consent of the client. It is for this reason that we encourage continual reference to the therapeutic contract. The patient is, at all times, free to exert "counter-control"—that is, to challenge, refute, or refuse to comply with the therapist's suggestions and negotiate a new contract. Thus, the therapist's influence is never disguised, as it is often wont to be in more traditional approaches. Moreover, as Bandura (1969, p. 85) stated, "In discussing moral and practical issues of behavioral control it is essential to recognize that social influence is not a question of imposing controls where none existed before. All behavior is inevitably controlled . . . and the process of behavior change . . . involves substituting new controlling conditions for those that have regulated a person's behavior." In considering the ethical implications of therapy as a social influence procedure, the criterion is one of promoting the client's freedom of choice—his choice of knowingly selecting certain modes of interacting with the world.

But what, students wonder, of the ethics of initiating treatment with the involuntary patient? Of attempting to prevent a potentially suicidal person from harming himself? Of committing a patient to a psychiatric hospital without his explicit consent? Such decisions are moral dilemmas. Where the person's behavior is harmful or potentially destructive to the freedom of others (for example, a father's sexual abuse of his children or a parent's battering of his child), some writers have suggested that the therapist must serve as a representative of the larger society in which he works. For example, Ullmann and Krasner (1965, p.42) stated that if "a person's behavior has become a burden to society and if his behavior can be changed, whether he wants it or not, it is right and proper to change the behavior." And they stated further (p. 43), "he (the therapist) may even have to admit that he is in a better position to know what is 'good' than a hospitalized (psychotic) patient or a child." In the case of a person intent on taking his own life, we believe that preventing him, if it is within our ability to do so by involuntary hospitalization, for instance, may eventually enhance the individual's freedom of choice, by permitting him to find alternative solutions. Where an individual's behavior violates legal codes (for example, chronic drug addicts, sexual deviates), the ethical dilemma becomes more complex. Conventional norms regarding the need to set limits on behavioral practices (for example, drug use, promiscuity) might be questioned. In such cases as these, we agree with Bandura (1971, p. 87) who stated that "therapeutic agents may support changes in socially prescribed directions or give legitimacy to deviant patterns, depending upon the social and personal consequences of the behavior, the client's preferences, and the therapist's own value orientation."

And finally, what about the ethical issues involved with charging a fee for therapy when some writers suggest that some treatment is productive of illness or at least of questionable efficacy? Here, we do believe that it is incumbent upon the therapist to demonstrate—at least with his own clients—that the services for which the client is paying are effective. By this we do not mean that change is entirely the responsibility of the therapist. However, we wish to stress the need for constant assessment and feedback regarding the process of therapy. We have stated the need for evaluation of planned interventions and for evaluation of outcome. It has been advocated by some practicing clinicians that if the therapist fails in his efforts to assist the client, all or some of the client's fees be refunded. We leave this decision to the individual therapist. We do maintain that the therapist who acknowledges himself as a professional whose services are to be paid for has a responsibility to demonstrate his competency as a change agent. We hope our guidelines for the process and evaluation of psychotherapy will assist the therapist in this purpose.

STRUCTURING INITIAL PSYCHOTHERAPY EFFORTS

It is often helpful to provide the client with a cognitive structure that will allow him to make sense out of the therapy experience before it occurs. Goldstein, Heller, and Sechrest (1966) hypothesized that:

1. A cognitive structure which enables an individual correctly to anticipate and organize his experience will facilitate learning and retention of new or more elaborate behavior sequences. (p. 240)

2. Giving patients prior information about the nature of psychotherapy, the theories underlying it, and the techniques to be used will facilitate progress in psychotherapy. (p. 245)

In the field of educational research, there is some evidence to suggest that stating specific objectives before teaching a lesson may enhance the speed and retention of learning (Mager, 1962). Rotter (1954) suggested a method of successive structuring over the course of therapy in which the patient is instructed in the rationale and purpose, goals and expectations of each successive phase of psychotherapy. Hoehn-Saric et al. (1964) discussed the systematic preparation of patients for psychotherapy. In their role-induction interview, they told the patient what could be expected in psychotherapy, how he was expected to behave, the therapist's expected behavior, realistic expectations of improvement, and how to recognize and overcome resistance. They reported significant positive effects on behavior within therapy and after therapy.

We have found that the central flow chart of this book (Figure 1) *can be shared with the client to structure each phase of treatment.* Both beginning therapists and clients find it a sensible sequence that helps them locate the specific tasks of each phase. It is *not* necessary to share each detail of the procedure, but an outline in general terms will be helpful to the client.

There are two parts to structuring initial change efforts. The first part involves the question, "What are the objectives of initial change efforts?" The second part involves the question, "How are these objectives to be accomplished?" We will now discuss each of these questions.

PLANNING BEHAVIOR CHANGE EFFORTS

There are several ways of conceptualizing behavior change. The target is always responses to situations and not merely responses.

1. *Response decrement* involves decreasing the frequency of an undesirable behavior in the client's repertoire.

2. *Response increment* involves increasing the frequency of a desirable behavior in the client's repertoire.

3. *Response acquisition* involves training a new behavior not currently in the client's repertoire.

4. *Cognitive restructuring* involves changing the client's characteristic ways of organizing his experience and generating alternatives.

We will list some procedures that have been used in each of these approaches. We do not intend to provide an exhaustive list nor to review the literature. Nor will we discuss the theoretical principles underlying the methods we describe. There is an inherent danger in listing techniques or methods for behavior change. We strongly agree with Bergin's (1971) conclusion that the study of the effectiveness of therapy needs to be based on the evaluation of specific methods applied to specific problems. But simply listing methods as we do below may seem to some readers to represent a superficial behavioral eclecticism, a conceptual format that misrepresents behavioral approaches to therapy. Our list may appear to take treatment interventions from different conceptual frameworks and treat them more or less equally. We may seem to imply that different treatment approaches cover nonoverlapping domains of behavior problems. In fact, many treatment interventions represent conflicting treatment models, which are often aimed at dealing with the same behavior problem, which are based on differentially validated notions, and which will probably be shown to be differentially effective. In short, our overview is far too uncritical and it may leave the reader with the impression that the choice of technique is a matter of personal taste, rather than dependent upon empirical support. Nothing could be further from the overall intention of this book.

We urge the reader to read beyond this book for an empirical comparison of interventions, for more description of the interventions, and for an understanding of the theoretical underpinnings of these interventions.

However, we have found that in treatment with a particular client it may be necessary to apply simultaneously more than one approach to a problem. For example, if a client avoids close interpersonal relationships this may require a desensitization procedure or a response acquisition procedure, or both. The first step in comparing therapy interventions is to begin with an effective intervention procedure. The procedure may have several components. The next step would be to study the components of the intervention by systematically dismantling the intervention to make an already effective procedure more efficient. In the process, something theoretical can be learned if the treatment components are grounded on different principles. We refer the reader to McFall and Twentyman (1973) for a pioneering series of studies which dismantles an intervention procedure for assertiveness training which was previously found to be effective (McFall and Marston, 1970).

Although discussion of each of these four general strategies for altering maladaptive behavior is presented individually, *in actual clinical practice, many techniques will be used in conjunction or successively*. You may employ systematic desensitization to reduce examination anxiety but discover that you also must include in the treatment program instruction in study skills, stimulus control techniques, and practice in assertive responses for talking with teachers and classmates. The full treatment program may include a variety of response decrement, response increment, response acquisition, and cognitive restructuring techniques.

Response Decrement

Systematic desensitization Systematic desensitization is used extensively as a means of counter-conditioning incapacitating *anxiety*, thereby reducing avoidance behavior and paving the way for more adaptive approach behavior. Before starting systematic desensitization it should be determined whether the client is avoiding a particular situation because of excessive anxiety or because he lacks the requisite skills to cope with that situation.

It is also important to determine precisely what relation avoidance has to the rest of the client's life. For example, a snake-phobic girl may also be avoiding a camping trip with her boyfriend because she fears interpersonal closeness.

In systematic desensitization, the patient and therapist construct a hierarchy of stimulus situations that elicit anxiety, proceeding from the least to the most anxiety-producing. The client is then taught progressive muscle relaxation (Jacobson, 1964) in which he is trained systematically to relax all of the major muscle groups throughout his body. Since relaxation is incompatible with anxiety, when the client is in a relaxed and comfortable state, he is asked to visualize the weakest item in his anxiety hierarchy of emotionally arousing scenes. If the client signals anxiety (usually by lifting an index finger), the scene is promptly withdrawn and relaxation is reinstated. The item is repeatedly presented until it ceases to elicit anxiety. If the client can visualize a scene without experiencing anxiety on the first presentation, the next item on the hierarchy is presented until, finally, the client can imagine each scene without experiencing discomfort. Generally, following systematic desensitization, some form of *in vivo* desensitization is employed in which the client is asked to experience in real-life or in laboratory simulation the heretofore feared object or situation. (The client is frequently asked to relax himself prior to the encounter.)

Systematic desensitization has proven extremely useful in the treatment of phobias as well as obsessive-compulsive disorders, psychosomatic disorders, frigidity, exhibitionism, insomnia, nightmares, and public speaking anxiety.

Covert sensitization   (See Cautela, 1966, 1967.) Covert sensitization is, in many ways, the reverse of desensitization since the goal is to encourage an avoidance response rather than encourage approach behavior.

Covert sensitization is used to treat undesirable, maladaptive behaviors typified by undesirably high approach rates such as in obesity, alcoholism, drug abuse, inappropriate sexual behavior, and so on. The client is first taught to relax as in the desensitization procedure. Then he is asked to visualize the events leading up to the initiation of the undesirable act. Just as he begins to engage in the undesirable response, he is instructed to imagine feeling sick to his stomach, or some other disagreeable event. After practicing these sequences in the therapist's office, under the therapist's close supervision so that the client does not learn to habituate to the noxious imagery, the client may be asked to continue self-administered treatment between visits.

The term "covert" refers to the fact that both the behavior to be decreased and the aversive stimuli to be associated with the behaviors are verbally described to the client by the therapist and the client is told to imagine the sequence of scenes. Sensitization is accomplished by associating the undesirable behavior with a vivid, exceedingly disagreeable consequence for short periods of exposure time. The client is requested to imagine himself as the "actor" in the scene, allowing himself to experience fully the sensations described. When instructed to terminate the undesirable behavior (in thought), the client frequently experiences a sensation of relief. Hence, termination of the maladaptive behavior is associated with positive reinforcement while emission of the behavior is symbolically associated with unpleasant, noxious cues.

Example (fictional): Ray Ugghill was an alcoholic of seven years. He wanted to to stop drinking since he was in danger of losing his third job. Covert sensitization was employed. Mr. Ugghill was told to close his eyes and concentrate on the scene the therapist described. He was told to picture himself reaching for and pouring a fresh, frosty glass of beer. As he swallows the drink, it tastes bitter and putrid. He feels nauseous and dizzy. His body trembles, his face sweats and suddenly he begins vomiting. The vomit pours over his new suit and falls into the beer and onto the table. People start moving away from him. He quickly puts the glass down and runs out of the bar, hoping to cool off his perspiration-drenched body. As soon as he reaches the street, he experiences a heavenly sense of relief. He feels calm and relaxed, his whole body feels alive and vigorous.

Flooding   (See Hogan and Kirchner, 1967; Stampfl and Levis, 1967). Flooding, like systematic desensitization, is used to reduce maladaptive avoidance behavior. This procedure has also been called "implosive" therapy. It is often preferred to systematic desensitization because, when applicable, it takes less time with equally efficacious results. Flooding is based on a classical extinction paradigm which states that in the absence of reinforcement, a response will decrease in frequency.

In this procedure, Valium (a tranquilizing drug) may be administered to the client four hours prior to the flooding session. During the session, which may last anywhere from one and a half to four hours, the client is repeatedly presented images of stimulus situations he has heretofore avoided because of subjective feelings of discomfort. There is no relief from the bombardment of unpleasant material; the client is not permitted to leave the room, despite his fears. Eventually, his discomfort is as high as it can be. Since the fear response does not get reinforced in reality (there is no real danger and avoidance behavior, such as leaving the situation, is not rewarded), fear eventually decreases. As soon as the fear completely dissipates, when presentation of the symptom-contingent cues no longer elicits anxiety (which may be monitored physiologically, for example, heart rate, GSR), the client is exposed to the actual feared objects.

Flooding has been used successfully with phobias and obsessive-compulsive behaviors. Long-time phobias have been extinguished in as few as three or four sessions using this procedure.

Example: Mrs. Carla Cassey was terrified of snakes which put a damper on her family's anticipated summer plans to take a two month camping trip across the United States. Not only couldn't she tolerate the thought of a snake, the very image of a reptile was sufficient to make her shudder with revulsion and terror. Careful questioning revealed that what Carla disliked most about reptiles was their blackness, their "slitheryness," and what she perceived as their sliminess. During the flooding sessions, which lasted two hours, she was asked to close her eyes and imagine herself alone in a deserted farmhouse. The place was dark and deserted; the plaster was falling from the ceiling, and the walls were punctuated by small holes. Suddenly, a snake slid out from one of the holes and wound his way toward Carla. In quick succession, snake after snake poured from the walls and woodwork, large snakes and small snakes, black snakes and speckled ones, wound their way around Carla's feet and arms and chest, approaching her neck and head. Carla screamed and cried, but there was no way out. The scene continued, getting increasingly more vivid and disgusting. Eventually, after the fourth presentation of the scene, Carla stopped reacting with fright. She ceased trembling and crying, and listened calmly to the descriptions. At the end of the session, she was shown and asked to handle a rubber model of a black snake. She did this easily. After two more flooding sessions, Carla was ready for her camping trip. (Case based on one seen by Dr. Fred Todd.)

Biofeedback   Biofeedback techniques are used to train people to increase their voluntary control over a variety of physiological functions. For example, with training, individuals can control their heart rates, alpha rhythms, and muscle tension voluntarily. Feedback techniques employ a kind of "physiological mirror" or psychophysiological feedback loop. By precisely detecting and monitoring a physiological event, such as heartbeat, and then converting the resulting electronic signal into either auditory or visual feedback, an individual can try various "internal experiments" to control the physiological event. Subjects may use internal control techniques such as thinking certain thoughts or systematically relaxing certain body parts. By receiving immediate feedback from the electronic monitor on the effectiveness of their "experiments," they can correct their behavior to attain the desired result.

The training method in biofeedback involves three requirements, according to Kamiya (in Barber *et al.*, 1971):

1. The physiological function to be brought under control must be continuously monitored with sufficient sensitivity to detect moment-by-moment changes.

2. Changes in the physiological measure must be reflected immediately to the subject (this is called "feedback").

3. The subject must be motivated to learn. (With humans, motivation is often sustained by giving the patient a quantitative score of his performance every few minutes.)

Physiological or *bio*feedback training has been used in the clinical treatment of tension headaches (Budzynski *et al.*, 1970), phobias (Budzynski and Stoyva, 1971), and a variety of stress-related disorders (Barber *et al.*, 1971). When biofeedback is employed in systematic desensitization, it aids in making relaxation more efficient (since there is immediate feedback to the therapist as well as to the patient on the extent of relaxation attained). Biofeedback is also helpful in monitoring arousal levels during visualization of anxiety-arousing scenes and as a method of providing quantitative data on the desensitization process.

Although biofeedback instruments are quite expensive, a variety of portable models are being marketed at moderate prices.

Example: A forty-three-year-old woman had been unable to learn muscle relaxation because of a marked inability to relax. She suffered from extreme social anxiety at social gatherings. At such times she also exhibited a tremor (functional in nature) of the right hand which prevented her from shaking hands with anyone or from even holding a glass. Feedback training was started with the frontalis (forehead) but this proved too frustrating. Using feedback from her forearm muscle (which is easier to control), she made good progress. Later the training was shifted to the masseter (jaws) and finally, back to the frontalis. After she had learned to relax well, her regular therapist desensitized her to social anxiety without the use of feedback devices. At the conclusion of treatment, she was able to participate in social events without trembling or undue anxiety. (Taken from Budzynski *et al.*, 1971.)

Negative practice   (See Dunlap, 1932; Lehrer, 1960.) Negative practice is useful in eliminating habits which the patient finds unadaptive by the active, deliberate massed practice of these habits. Negative practice is based on the theory that effortful activity eventually generates a negative drive state called "reactive inhibition." Under conditions of massed practice of, for instance, an hour or more, reactive inhibition builds up rapidly, reducing the likelihood of the occurrence of the response in the future. Under conditions of arousal and dissipation of the reactive inhibition, there develops a conditioned inhibition or negative habit of not responding. Important to the success of this technique are the motivation of the patient to eradicate the behavior, the knowledge of a correct alternative response, the similarity of the habit as practiced in massed practice sessions with that in real life, and the elimination of factors that might maintain the undesirable response.

Negative practice is useful in such disorders as stammering, tics, thumb-sucking, nail-biting, and exhibitionism.

Example (fictional): Mr. Boxer, a salesman, was disturbing his employer, his wife and children, and his customers, by his repetitive, irritating throat-clearing. He could barely utter five words in succession without pausing to clear his throat. Mr. Boxer was well motivated to rid himself of this unpleasant habit which by now had become automatic. The therapist scheduled forty-five-minute sessions in which Mr. Boxer was required to clear his throat repetitively, while reading a passage, with a minimum of 100 throat-clearings per session. In five sessions, with home practice interspersed, Mr. Boxer had markedly decreased his habit and in a month had almost completely eliminated it.

Aversive counter-conditioning   Some behaviors that have strongly gratifying immediate consequences have serious long-term consequences, such as alcoholism, excessive use of drugs, smoking, or certain sexual behaviors that the client wishes to change such as transvestism, exhibitionism, or fetishism. One way of reducing the incidence of the "problem" behavior is to change the consequences contingent on producing the behavior. However, if the stimuli eliciting the behavior remain the same, such as the sight of beer or certain fetishistic objects, changing the consequences will have only short-term effectiveness, at best. Therefore, it is useful to associate the *eliciting stimuli* with noxious or aversive properties, thereby reducing the likelihood of the response. The general procedure by which this is accomplished is called "aversive counter-conditioning" (based on a classical conditioning paradigm).

The rationale of aversive counter-conditioning is based on the fact that an object or activity that is repeatedly associated with negative (painful, uncomfortable, aversive) properties will acquire some of the negative properties of the aversive stimulus. The individual will therefore come to avoid the object or activity.

Among the aversive agents used in aversive counter-conditioning are nauseous pharmacological agents, such as apomorphine or emerine, aversive electrical stimulation (shock), and recently, symbolically induced aversion (where positively valued events are repeatedly associated with strong verbally presented descriptions of nauseous feelings, revolting experiences, or painful sensations).

In aversive counter-conditioning, it is often necessary to provide "booster" sessions at intervals of either six months or a year, following the successful counter-conditioning, since over time the negative associations can extinguish in the absence of reinforcement. A useful account and critique of the current status of aversive conditioning may be found in Rachman and Teasdale's book *Aversion Therapy and Behavior Disorders: An Analysis* (1969).

Example (fictional): Joe Porter, a thirty-five-year-old married man, masturbated each evening to fetishistic fantasies revolving around angora sweaters. His wife was quite upset by Joe's behavior and their sex life had become one of marked abstinence. Joe finally decided to seek treatment for his difficulty. Aversion therapy was begun. Joe was asked to engage in his usual fantasies but to signal (raise his hand) when the fetishistic object (angora sweaters) was clearly visualized. At that time a strong shock was administered to his forearm. This procedure was repeated daily over two weeks. When Joe had difficulty summoning up images of angora sweaters, real angora sweaters, as well as pictures of them were introduced into the sessions.

Other response decrement procedures Extinction refers here to a measurable decrease in response probability, that is, a response decrement. It may be brought about in several ways. Preventing the occurrence of a response by nonrewarding it or blocking it may result in the decline in frequency of a maladaptive behavior over time. Explanations of extinction may be couched in the form of inhibitory theories or interference theories. Extinction itself, however, simply refers to a description, rather than an explanation, of a behavioral phenomenon, namely, response decrement. Similarly, reinforcing a new response as an alternative to the conditioned stimulus or discriminative stimulus may result in lessened likelihood of the old response.

One means of effecting extinction of an undesirable response is through the judicious use of *punishment*. Punishment is here defined as response-contingent procedures which result in a deceleration of behavior (and hopefully, eventually, extinction). The use of punishment may be indicated in the following situations:

1. When positive reinforcement inevitably accompanies the emission of a specific inappropriate behavior.

2. When a behavior is dangerous to self or others.
3. When a behavior seriously interferes with learning.

There is no fail-proof manner of determining a suitable punishment for an individual in the absence of objective observation and experimentation. For example, some children find that being restricted to the house is rewarding since it enables them to gain time alone with a parent or play with desirable toys. One way of selecting "punishing events" is by observing what an individual *avoids* when behaving freely.

Although punishment procedures are often ineffectual and result merely in the suppression, rather than elimination of behavior, if applied appropriately, they can be quite useful. It is essential, for instance, that administration of the punishing event occur while the client is performing the undesirable act (for example, smacking his sister) or as soon as possible after it is discovered (in other words, the oft-repeated sanction "Wait until Father gets home!" is ineffective in decreasing the likelihood of an undesired behavior in the future). Punishment procedures that prevent an individual from performing "restitution" or from making alternative pro-social responses (such as excessively long periods of solitary confinement or physical abuse) are similarly likely to be ineffectual. It is important when considering the use of punishment to decide upon and facilitate the development of desirable alternative behaviors.

Punishment techniques that have been used extensively and often successfully include temporary placement in a less reinforcing environment (time out from positive reinforcement and isolation), removal of tokens, points, or money (fines or losing privileges), physical restraints (used, for example, in dealing with self-injurious behavior such as head-banging), and restrictions from engaging in desired activities.

Example (fictional): Six-year-old Marvin loved to tease four-year-old Sally by snatching away her favorite doll. To decrease this "doll-snatching" behavior, Marvin's parents adopted a time-out procedure. If they saw "mischievous Marv" grabbing sister's doll, they immediately sent him to his room for a five-minute time-out period. When he returned, they suggested a toy he might play with and praised any appropriate independent or cooperative activity he showed.

Response Increment

The basic assumption with response increment procedures is that the desired behavior is in the client's repertoire (at least occurs sometimes to some degree) and that the frequency of the response can be increased by either stimulus control or contingency management. The goal is to accelerate the frequency of the desired response.

There are times when the best method of changing behavior is altering the environment in which the person functions. This is particularly true when dealing with chronic inpatients, mentally retarded individuals, autistic children, large groups of institutionalized persons, and children. Environmental manipulation is, by no means, limited to these populations. It can occur on a small scale by setting up a point program for a youngster who refuses to do his homework or help with household chores, or an adolescent who constantly abuses automobile and late-hour privileges. An entire token economy program can also be set up for a ward of hospitalized inpatients. Making small changes in the home environment such as changing the discriminative stimuli prompting certain behaviors can have profound effects on such behaviors as eating, studying, sleeping, and so forth. The following pages will deal with suggestions for implementing modifications in the environment in the service of changing maladaptive behavior.

Token Systems   Token systems involve changing the reinforcement contingencies maintaining behavior. They may be used to extinguish maladaptive behavior or to strengthen the occurrence of more appropriate behavior. In order to establish a token system, it is first necessary to determine what reinforcements are controlling the behavior you want to alter. For example, it may be the case that crazy gesticulating and bizarre verbalizations are reinforced by ward personnel with increased attention while quiet, cooperative behavior is ignored (or is not positively commented on). Similarly, it may be that a patient bites, kicks, and screams in order to be locked in the seclusion room because she finds the privacy of seclusion a desirable, reinforcing experience. One cannot assume that one knows what is reinforcing to people a *priori* (or, "One man's meat is another man's poison"). Generally, a good rule of thumb to go by is that what is reinforcing to the individual tends to occur in high frequency (for example, smoking, watching television). Bradfield (1970) suggests six ways that have proven helpful in selecting or establishing effective reinforcers:

    1. Ask the client what he likes or wants. If the client repeatedly chooses expensive or unavailable reinforcers (such as a new car, a date with Jane Fonda), the therapist might provide a "reinforcement menu" listing the available reinforcers and allow the client to select from these.

    2. Observe the client's behavior in situations when many alternative behaviors are possible. For instance, if when alone, a child repeatedly decides to play with his model railroad, it is likely that *this* activity is reinforcing for *this* child.

    3. A method for establishing reinforcers is Ayllon and Azrin's (1968) "reinforcer sampling." The client is instructed or permitted to engage in events that he might find enjoyable. If the behavior engaged in is enjoyable, then similar events may be used to reinforce other less probable behaviors.

    4. Positive attention (such as praise, touch, smiles, congratulatory words like "good") from adults and peers is a *potential* reinforcer. Attention is cheap, powerful, and in limitless supply, although too often, people are stingy supplying it or it is misguidedly used to maintain undesirable behaviors.

    5. Potential reinforcers may be selected by experimenting with objects and events which are valued positively by a large number of others. A warning is

necessary here, since clients who display maladaptive behavior often have strange reinforcement histories. Consequently, it is often difficult to predict what will be uniquely reinforcing for *them* based on knowledge of others. The best course is to try various reinforcers until one is found which demonstrably alters behavior.

6. Finally, when dealing with groups of individuals, it is useful to establish conditioned reinforcers such as stars, poker chips, points, coins that may be traded in for any of a wide variety of other objects or events (called "back-up reinforcers"), any one of which might be reinforcing to some members of the group. In classrooms, for instance, a certain number of points may be necessary to gain access to the "play area" which contains a wide selection of games, craft supplies, blocks, and the like. In institutional token programs, a "store" is often created where a wide array of objects may be "purchased" with tokens.

Some guidelines for the establishment of token programs are given below:

1. *Baseline data* should be gathered to determine the frequency of behavior, the events which form a setting for the behavior's occurrence, and the consequences of the behavior under "natural," that is, preintervention conditions.

2. When it is clearly understood which behaviors are to be extinguished and which responses are to be strengthened, *reinforcers must be selected* that are sufficiently powerful and durable to maintain the new behaviors over time. It may be necessary to shape successive approximations of the response if it is one that has never been learned by the individual. It may be necessary to use a modeling procedure to teach the response to the patient.

3. *Reinforcement* for the occurrence of a low frequency or new response is best made quickly contingent on the behavior—the longer the delay between the response and the reinforcement, the less the likelihood of strengthening the behavior. It may be that the reinforcer is not powerful enough, or that the patient can get the reinforcement in ways other than the desired behavior. In successful token programs, social reinforcers or the individual's own satisfaction with his new responses become sufficient to maintain the behavior even in the absence of the initial or primary reinforcer.

4. The individual(s) in the token program should be carefully informed of the new contingencies—what is expected of them, what reinforcers may be earned by exhibiting the behavior, when they will receive the reinforcers, and how much they can earn by each behavior. Careful charting should accompany the institution of the program in order to see if it is having the desired effect and to allow the therapist to investigate when it is not.

5. *Shaping:* The desired behavior is shaped by successive approximations in very much the same way as in the traditional operant paradigm.

The design and implementation of token programs can become complex and sophisticated, approaching the creation of a new culture and economy. The preceding description is only a sketch of what needs to be done in the simplest programs. For a more comprehensive discussion of token systems, see Ayllon and Azrin (1968).

Example: Token System for an Adult. Betty White, a thirty-four-year-old hospitalized, psychotically depressed woman, was spending her entire time in the hospital lying on her bed or sleeping. She avoided all social encounters, refused to participate in occupational or recreational therapy, and insisted that meal trays be brought to her room where she dined alone. Ward personnel decided that Betty's present behavior was destructive to her and would not help her depression. They felt Betty should be spending at least eight hours out of bed, should attend ward activities and socialize, at least minimally, with other patients and staff. They observed that the one activity Betty engaged in with high frequency was smoking and drinking coffee. She also requested sleeping medication each evening. It was decided to make these reinforcers contingent upon time-off-bed, responding to the questions of staff and patients, and attending activities. If she wanted to buy time on her bed for naps, she would have to pay for them with tokens earned by engaging in the preceding behaviors. A token program was established with Betty, giving the token value of each appropriate behavior and the cost of each activity they wanted to extinguish. All staff personnel were notified of the treatment program and were instructed to reward Betty immediately upon making the desired responses (that is, receiving three tokens each time she went to occupational therapy) with the other patients or walked down to the dining room for meals. She was required to pay for meals served to her in her room. In one week, Betty's behavior improved significantly. She received considerable positive feedback from other patients who congratulated her on her sociability and began to invite her more frequently to join them on off-ward events. Betty herself began feeling more "competent" as she saw her behavior visibly paying off and began talking about her plans for the future.

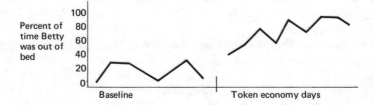

Percent of time Betty was out of bed

Baseline   Token economy days

Example: Token System for a Child. Mrs. Bernstein complained of the irresponsible behavior of her thirteen-year-old son William. She said she had to spend most of her time "being his maid." She was also concerned about his behavior at school. He was continuously in trouble with his teachers. Mrs. Bernstein said that William eventually got his way because it "gave her a headache to argue with him." William said his problems at school were due to his difficulty in communicating with his mother. He said she had time for everybody else in the community but him. He complained that he was always talking to her "on the run." He said it was important for him to have money but that he could easily get "loans" from his older sisters. The family agreed to set up a token economy with payoffs being money, praise from mother, and time to talk to her when she wasn't doing something else.

The following point system was set up, with penalty points for certain events, and token cards punched by the mother. Each point was to be redeemable in money (a penny a point, each token card 25¢), or in time with the mother (5 cards = 15 minutes). In addition to this, William was praised for his work by his mother.

Activity	Point Value	Penalty
1. Making bed	2	-
2. Brushing teeth	2	-
3. Shower or bath	2	-
4. Practice piano	5	-
5. Hang up clothes (upstairs)	2	-
6. Bring clothes downstairs to wash	2	-
7. Take out trash	10	-
8. Feed the dog	3	
9. Turn out lights in room	2	2
10. Wash socks and gym clothes	3	2
11. Vacuum basement steps	5	-
12. Vacuum dining room	10	-
13. Vacuum living room	10	-
14. Wipe up around carpet (damp mop)	5	-
15. Clean room on inspection	10	-
16. Any good report from school or good grade	20	8 (bad report)

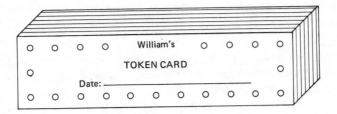

The mother's attitude toward William changed. She said, "I enjoy talking with him now." William liked the point system, and his behavior in school improved once he had "worn off" the stigma he had developed with some of his teachers.

Example: Token System for Groups. The University of Colorado Medical Center's day care psychoeducational facility for emotionally disturbed children uses a token economy for conflict management during a thirty-minute play period. A child who played by himself for a ten-minute period without disrupting the play of other children earns one point. If two children play together, both children earn two points for the ten-minute period. The number of points each child earns equaled the number of children involved in the play. Conflict might arise but children are not penalized as long as they manage the conflict. They can also call for help from an adult but it would cost each child a point for the "consultation." Points are redeemable (when a child earns over 100 points) at a penny a point and a trip is arranged to a department store so that children can spend their money. Some children pool their points to buy more expensive games.

In this situation, withdrawn children began to play with other children, acting-out problems diminished greatly, "psychotic" symptoms reduced greatly, and many children developed skills in leadership and handling conflict.

The therapists were able to use the points creatively. For example, they told a child who had been withdrawn, "You only got one point today. In here you win points for playing with other kids." Then when the child looked interested in a game with some other kids, the therapists said "I'll give each kid in this group ten extra points if they can include Judy in this game for the next ten minutes." The children said, "Oh, boy," and tried to include Judy. The following week Judy asked *them* if she could play with them. At first, the therapists reinforced any inclusion, but gradually they said, "I don't think Judy is really playing this game," and were gradually able to increase the quality of Judy's participation and of the interaction of others with her.

The therapists could also teach skills in conflict management by using the act of dispensing points. For example, they would roam about in the group and observe, "I don't see this group handling things too well. Jake is punching Ted over there, and Steve is sulking. What about that? If you expect to get six points each you had better handle that in the next few minutes." The group would pull together, quickly talk about the disruptions, and continue with game.

One of the fundamental but all too infrequently discussed parts of the token economy is the need for the economy to operate on a base of *power.* This is true in a family or in any institutional setting utilizing an economy. No economy can work, for example, if it is easy to obtain the same rewards without doing what the economy requires. With a child this may involve the use of *time out* procedures. *Time out* is a technical term that describes one kind of withdrawal of reinforcement. With children it is usually accompanied by social exclusion in a place of low stimulation for a period of time which can be extended until the obstreperous behavior ceases. It is sometimes effective with children to suggest that they have ten minutes to decide whether they will participate or continue on time out. A few children find time out quite bearable. Again, with all children the economy must find its power base to be effective. Token programs must also be evaluated frequently so that individuals do not "satiate" with the available reinforcers, so that hoarding does not develop, and so that additional adaptive behaviors can be added once the older ones become stabilized and maintained by social reinforcers. For instance, over time, the "price" of certain reinforcers may be raised so that more of the appropriate behavior is required in order to earn the same amount of reinforcement. While token programs are not panaceas for response increment, they can be a very effective tool if used creatively.

Environment shifts With many clients, environmental shifts may be appropriate, particularly those clients seen in community mental health centers, lower socioeconomic neighborhoods, and psychiatric hospitals. Emotional difficulties may be exacerbated and directly related to impossible living conditions, real financial stress, deviant peer cultures that reinforce drug addiction and prostitution, lack of vocational skills, and so on. Just as you cannot talk therapy to a starving man, it makes little sense to try to correct behavior that is perpetuated by an overwhelming home environment. It is first necessary to change the environment. This may involve the difficult task of organizing the community at its grass roots (Alinsky, 1971). A variety of social agencies, welfare offices, vocational rehabilitation offices, community-based organizations, halfway houses, drug and alcohol rehabilitation centers may also provide useful services for a particular case. The therapist should be informed about the social agencies in his community, the services they provide, requirements for their use, and their general operating procedures. The therapist may need to decide whether a case-by-case approach is sensible when a common set of community-based problems are the root causes of a large proportion of referrals.

Many children and adolescents live in homes where sexual acting out is not only tolerated, but encouraged; where alcoholism and physical abuse are common; where parents are severely emotionally disturbed. Often, foster or temporary placement is a choice worth considering. On the other hand, individuals with similar kinds of difficulties, such as abusers of drugs and drink, may make superior recoveries when living with groups of people familiar with the experience and treatment of these difficulties, though treatment methods such as Synanon and Daytop Village have yet to be evaluated in terms of effectiveness.

Concepts of the therapeutic community or milieu treatment are also based on the premise that the environment determines the incidence of both adaptive and maladaptive behavior. For instance, the simple act of having nurses dress in everyday clothing rather than white uniforms changes the expectations of patients on a psychiatric ward. The message being communicated by the hospital to the patient is: "You are not 'ill' and 'irresponsible' and do not require solicitous and, at times, infantile attention. Rather, you have problems in living that we, as other individuals, can help you with. The major burden is on yourself." Similarly, permitting patients to take major responsibility for significant decisions in their hospital course, such as when to take a pass, for how long, whether to participate in certain activities, and so on, communicates to the patient that the staff views him as competent and capable of handling his own affairs. "Never do for the patient what he can do for himself" is a useful rule to observe both in institutional and outpatient therapy.

Stimulus Control   Major environmental changes are not always necessary to affect behavior profoundly. Stimulus control techniques have been found useful in interrupting and/or establishing competing response chains. Fox (1962) developed a program to improve the studying habits of college students. One student, for example, was requested to go to the library at a specified time with only those books necessary for his physics course. He was assigned to a specific room and was told to leave the library immediately if he experienced discomfort or started to daydream. By doing this, the likelihood of receiving reinforcement for behaviors other than studies in a particular context is lessened. The essential element of these and similar programs is to arrange the environment so that difficulties and distractions are minimized in performing the required task. Often, marked behavioral changes can result from altering the stimulus conditions under which behavior usually occurs. One can decide that all studying is to occur at a desk in a room empty of other people, at a specified daily time and for a specified number of hours. Factors other than stimulus control are operating here. For example, isolation from people when studying prevents one from getting reinforced for doing things other than studying. However, it is possible that the desk and other associated stimuli will become discriminative for studying rather than entertainment, horseplay, or daydreaming (Goldiamond, 1965). Ferster, Nurnberger, and Levitt (1962) demonstrated how individuals could learn to structure their environment in order to reduce the incidence of overeating. Stimulus control was employed as part of the total program. Eating, for example, was permitted to occur only in a designated place, at specified times. Stuart (1972) encouraged clients desiring to lose weight to remove food from all places in the house other than the kitchen and to purchase only foods requiring preparation. Restricting eating responses to a special table covered with a purple tablecloth in a certain room can have a dramatic effect on the self-control of eating (Goldiamond, 1965) if this is part of a total program designed to break the link between eating and socializing.

Self-control of a large number of behaviors, such as smoking, drinking, eating, sleeping, studying, practicing, and so on, can result from considering as part of the treatment both altering the stimulus conditions governing behavior and narrowing and defining the context in which behavior may occur.

Reciprocal Contracts   Lederer and Jackson (1968) and Stuart (1969), are among the many behaviorally oriented therapists who discussed the use of contracts as a way of programming behavioral change between spouses, families, and an adolescent and his parents. In reciprocal contracts, each party specifies what behaviors he would like to see the other party modify or increase. In return, he agrees to comply with the other party's requests concerning changes in his own behavior, or promises some special reinforcement. Contract requests should pass the "dead man's test," that is, requests should be for accelerating behaviors, a request for more of something rather than less (for example, not less bitching, less complaining, less fishing with "the boys"). Since nobody can perform less of anything than a dead man, the rule is readily applied! Stuart (1969) emphasized that each party in the contract should keep records on the desirable behaviors of the other in order to see how the contract is operating, and whether it needs modification. It may also be useful to include a behavioral sanction in the contract, for either failing to meet the terms of the agreement or for successfully meeting them for several weeks. A sanction would be a special consequence agreed upon by the parties beforehand to handle special contingencies of the contract.

Contracts may be useful adjuncts to therapy with hostile teen-agers who are warring with their parents. Rather than fight with the adolescent, ask him for his demands, that is, discover what he does want. When his requests are known, they may be negotiated with his parents and the therapist can help the family work out what obligations must be met in order for the adolescent to have his demands realized. Such behavioral contracting can often start a useful dialogue between parent and child, replacing acrimonious condemnations and/or defiant silence. Contracts are also useful with marital problems. They help specify the needs of each person and the payoffs for conforming with the contract. Negotiating a contract is also useful to the therapist in pinpointing dysfunctional means of communication during the negotiation process.

Example: Susie Grant, an independent but impulsive fifteen-year-old girl, kept running away from home for days at a time, ditched school repeatedly, and attacked her parents for their "muddle-headed, middle-class" ways. After she was picked up by the police for the third time, reciprocal contracting was employed with Susie and her parents. Mr. and Mrs. Grant were rather rigid, elderly people who were shocked by Susie's language and disrespect. They were reluctant to permit later hours and more freedom to Susie but were helped to realize that in the present situation, they were getting far less than what they desired. When Susie was asked for her demands, she replied: "Independence! More allowance! Less housework!" Her parents agreed to raise Susie's allowance by $5 weekly and allow her out in the evenings to 9:30 P.M. on weekdays and 11:30 P.M. on weekends in exchange for "polite" replies to their questions (being told, for example, where Susie planned to be and what she planned to do when she was out), punctuality at meals and in the evenings, and regular school attendance (to be monitored by having Susie request her teachers to sign a daily class attendance record).

Example: A contingency contract negotiated between a husband and wife had the *temporary* objective of providing a minimal polite relationship during the problem assessment phase of therapy. The contract was posted on the refrigerator.

We, the undersigned, in order to form a more perfect union, do hereby agree and contract to:

1. Neither make nor give any general summaries of the other's behavior. This to include:
   A. no accusations
   B. no ascribing of motive
2. Talk neither of separation nor of any future qualitative possibility, that is, no discussion of future quality of life until the May 15 meeting.
3. In discussion of problems, stick to a (the) specific situation, making sure by appropriate questions that the other understands *exactly* what is meant, that is, that each is discussing the same specific situation.
4. If appropriate, analyze moment by moment how or why any argument, discord, or misunderstanding arose.
5. And, in regard to (3) and (4) above, to validate the discussion of each by each communicating his or her understanding of the other, allowing that understanding to be corrected.
6. Allow each a time in the evening to:
   A. be alone
   B. for trivia
   C. relax
   D. talk of events of day
7. Not press a discussion if the other resists discussion. If this situation should arise, each will have the right to ask for an appointed time, with negotiable time limits, when problems that one or the other thinks important will be discussed. The party of whom an appointed time is requested must grant it.

Payoff for husband at end of month: New pipe, up to $10.00
Payoff for wife at end of month: New records, up to $10.00

_____	_____
(husband)	(wife)
_____	_____
(date)	(date)

Response Acquisition

Shaping   Shaping by successive approximations is often useful in teaching a new response. In the procedure, the desired total response is broken down into a series of smaller steps which are necessary for mastery of the final response. Each smaller response is reinforced until it is under the client's control. Gradually, more and more accurate approximations of the final response are required before reinforcement is delivered, until gradually, the entire response is learned. For example, in teaching a child to use a fork properly, reinforcement may be initially given for simply holding the fork in the right hand. Later, reinforcement may be made contingent on the child's bringing the fork in the proximity of his mouth, then inserting the fork into his mouth, then using the fork to pick up food and put it in his mouth, and so on. The idea is: Don't wait for a perfect execution before dispensing reinforcement. During training, reinforce each small successful approximation of the desired terminal behavior!

Modeling or observational learning   It is not always necessary to actively or immediately display behavior in order to learn new behavior patterns. Much of our learning is accomplished symbolically and through observation of others, rather than through immediate rehearsal. Modeling may be employed to teach new behaviors by providing the opportunity for the client to observe both the behavior and consequences that accrue to another individual without taking an immediate risk himself. As such, modeling may serve either to inhibit or disinhibit previously learned responses as well as teach new ones. Several factors serve to determine the extent to which modeling will occur: The characteristics of the model relative to the observer (the more similar they are, the greater the likelihood of imitation), attention-directing variables (the client's notice of the model's behavior), the discriminability of modeling stimuli of the behavior, and incentive or motivational factors. The reader is referred to Bandura and Walters (1963) and Bandura (1971) for a description of some of the factors the therapist should attend to when using modeling.

Example (fictional): Seven-year-old Billy Brown was frightened his first day at the ocean. He had never seen an ocean before; he only had experience in small wading pools in people's back yards. Upon seeing the waves roar and roll up to the shore, he imagined himself being gobbled up alive and pulled out to sea. He lingered at the shore several minutes, watching smaller children play fearlessly in the water. He even observed a five-year-old girl swimming merrily with her tube. Eventually, he edged closer and closer to the water and, finally, followed a boy of his own age into the waves.

Role Playing   Role playing or behavioral rehearsal is a tool that may be employed in a variety of therapeutic contexts—groups, marital or family therapy, individual therapy, laboratories on interpersonal communication or human relations—with useful results. Role playing provides the opportunity to "try on" new responses in simulated situations without risking failure; it provides the opportunity for self-correction and feedback from others; it permits the anticipation of difficult encounters and the rehearsal of ways of handling them; it allows members of different racial and ethnic groups to appreciate the feelings and experiences of individuals in other minorities.

Example: Jeanne, a sixteen-year-old girl, was describing her problem to her group. She was depressed and somewhat ashamed of her feelings but felt powerless to change. She said that her father had recently injured himself severely in an automobile accident. His entire jaw was broken, necessitating the shaving off of his beard, the mark of identity by which Jeanne had come to recognize him since she was an infant. Jeanne felt disgusted with and distant from her father with his bare face and bandaged jaw. She did not want to look at him or speak with him but realized that her attitude might further exacerbate an already difficult situation. The therapists suggested she role play a dialogue with her father in order to better understand her own feelings and to facilitate handling the situation at home. Jeanne did so and reported feeling better afterwards. She said she learned that her father could probably accept and understand her reactions without feeling defensive and that her speaking with him, rather than avoiding him, might reduce the distance she experienced.

Assertiveness training   Assertiveness training teaches clients more effective and adaptive means of dealing with others in their environment. To encourage greater assertiveness Salter (1949) described six skills he encouraged patients to private: expression of feelings ("feeling talk"), facial expressions to show feelings, use of the word "I," agreement with praise, training in contradiction or expressing differences of opinion, and, finally, spontaneity of expression.

There are several aspects of assertiveness training. The client is encouraged to recognize that he has *rights* as a human being—the right to make certain decisions for himself, the right not to be unfairly abused by others, the right to express his thoughts, and so forth. Often, the client is given small homework assignments to practice bits of assertive behavior: returning an unwanted shirt, insisting on a refund for a leaky container of milk, refusing to let someone sneak in ahead of him on a theatre line. Behavioral rehearsal is often employed in order to practice assertive responses in the security of the therapist's office before attempting them in real life.

Assertiveness training groups have been conducted (Rathus, 1972) in which clients are given practice in assertive speech (that is, demanding their rights), feeling talk (that is, expressing their likes and dislikes spontaneously), greeting talk, disagreeing passively and actively, agreeing with compliments, avoiding justifying each opinion, and looking people directly in the eye when speaking. These behaviors are a small sample of the kinds of response that might be taught in an assertiveness training program for a client.

Frequently assertiveness training is useful in treating depression where the patient often blames himself for mistakes in judgment when the more appropriate target might be a wife or husband, a fiance or friend.

Example: Dorothy, an eighteen-year-old college girl, entered therapy extremely anxious and depressed. She came to the office at the suggestion of her parents who complained of her constant hair-pulling, resulting in loss of hair and general untidiness. When Dorothy was alone with the therapist, she revealed that she was terrified of her upcoming marriage with her fiance, a youth of twenty-three, who was tyrannical and often irrational with her. He insisted that she cut off ties with her girlfriends and spend time with no one but him. He rejected the notion of equality in marriage and referred to Dorothy as his "slave." He repeatedly told Dorothy that "if she really loved him, she would do as he said." Dorothy, a timid, painfully shy girl who spoke in a near whisper, was given practice in assertiveness training. She was lectured on the absurdity of John's views—no one has the right to expect another person to relinquish her own rights to select friends and career. Then, Dorothy took turns playing John and herself in scenes in which she challenged his assumptions and refused to go along with his irrational requests. These practice sessions were tape-recorded and Dorothy criticized her own performance. As she experienced success in standing up to John, Dorothy became less depressed. She eventually decided to break her engagement and continue her college career.

McFall and Marston (1970) presented an effective standardized semiauto-mated assertiveness training program utilizing behavior rehearsal techniques with college students. The client practices responding to situations such as the following:

> *Narrator:* In this scene picture yourself standing in a ticket line outside a theater. You've been in line now for at least ten minutes, and it's getting pretty close to show time. You're still pretty far from the beginning of the line, and you're starting to wonder if there will be enough tickets left. There you are, waiting patiently, when two people walk up to the person in front of you and they begin talking. They're obviously all friends, and they're going to the same movie. You look quickly at your watch and notice that the show starts in just two minutes. Just then, one of the newcomers says to his friend in line:
> *Newcomer:* "Hey, the line's a mile long. How 'bout if we cut here with you?"
> *Person in line:* "Sure, come on. A couple more won't make any difference."
> *Narrator:* And as the two people squeeze in the line between you and their friend, one of them looks at you and says:
> *Newcomer:* "Excuse me. You don't mind if we cut in, do you?"
> (Bell sounds as cue for *S* to respond.)

Problem situations were sampled from a domain of over 2000 situations such as friends are interrupting your studying, the laundry has lost your cleaning, the waiter brings you a steak that is too rare, your boss asks you to work overtime when you already have plans. In the first training session the subject heard a recorded playback of his response in a feedback condition and was presented with an outline of several factors to consider in evaluating his response. For example, "Was my response direct and to the point? How was my tone of voice, inflection, communication of affect?" He was instructed to try improving his response on the three subsequent trials.

In the second training session the interactions were escalated. After the problem situation was described, a moderately assertive response plus a rebuttal by the antagonist were added and then the subject was asked to supply his response.

Task analysis   Gagné (1967) suggested a method for dismantling the desired terminal behavior into a hierarchy of subtasks. Tasks may then be broken down in terms of their complexity (the hierarchy goes from least to most complex), or in terms of sequence (the hierarchy goes from what to do first to what to do last), or in terms of prerequisites (the hierarchy goes from what skill must be acquired first to the terminal behavior).

If a terminal behavior is analyzed in terms of prerequisite skills, the hierarchy may be tested as follows. Suppose that behavior A is the terminal objective and that behavior B is a prerequisite skill for behavior A, and behavior C is a prerequisite skill for behavior B. This can be diagrammed as follows:

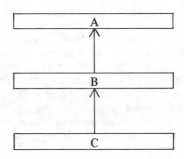

Suppose five subjects are tested to see if they have behaviors A, B, and C in their repertoires.

Hypothetical Distribution of Skills (X)
For Three Behaviors

Subjects	Behavior			Subjects	Behavior		
	A	B	C		A	B	C
1	X	X	X	1	X	X	X
2	X	X	X	2	X	X	X
3		X	X	3		X	X
4		X		4			X
5		X		5			X

On the left we see that subjects 4 and 5 can do B but cannot do C. This is a violation of the hierarchical picture above. On the right of the table we see the behaviors rearranged to show that the proper hierarchy is as follows:

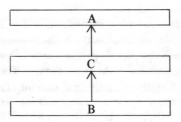

The procedure is analogous to Guttman scaling in questionnaire design. Of the procedure for testing a proposed task analysis, Gagné (1967) wrote:

> I fully realize that the type of analysis suggested . . . is not traditional. . . . But it seems to be in essence what is required in order to draw the desired conclusions about curriculum sequence. Perhaps someone with greater facility in quantitative analysis than I will be able to give it a greater elegance. (p. 33)

Once a task analysis has been performed, specific interventions can be programmed for skill acquisition using techniques of reinforcement, modeling, coaching, feedback, rehearsal, and other basic principles of learning theory.

Programmed learning In programmed instruction the student is an active learner who learns at his own pace and whose learning is shaped by feedback in a step-by-step fashion. The step size should be suitably small so that progress is possible and the learning experience is mostly a success experience.

Most programmed learning follows the diagram below:

Step 1
Step 2   Information
Step 3   provided
Step 4   Response
Step 5   required
Step 6

At each step progressively less information is provided and a progressively more complete response is required. Learning is organized from discrimination learning, to paired associate learning, to concept learning, to principle or rule learning, to the learning of problem-solving skills.

An excellent guide to writing programmed instructional units using the medium of the printed page is Espich and Williams (1967).

Summary of response acquisition methodology Usually a performance discrepancy analysis (see Sections A–D of Figure 1) will mean specifying how the client is behaving and feeling in a set of situations and specifying what the expectations (self and other) are for his behavior in those situations. A psychological test or other assessment procedure can be considered to give us a sampling of the client's behavior in some situations which may be simulations of the problem situations.

If we list those situations which are problematic for the client, we can then engage in a sequence of activities that has the benefit of merging assessment with intervention. First, we assess the client's performance in a random sample of problem situations (or simulations of these situations). Then we define what "competent" performance would be in those situations. The intervention program involves the use of practice in situations taken from the problem situation domains. Follow-up is an assessment of performance on other situations in the domain after treatment, and follow-up should include an assessment of the transfer of training. These steps can be described in a flow chart (see Section H21 of Figure 1 for an example).

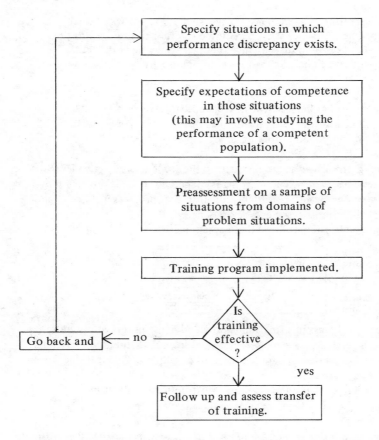

Figure 6.1.   Flow chart summarizing response acquisition methodology.

The flow chart below summarizes the training condition of an important experiment designed to assess the effectiveness of a semiautomated response acquisition program in interpersonal skills (Goldsmith, 1973).

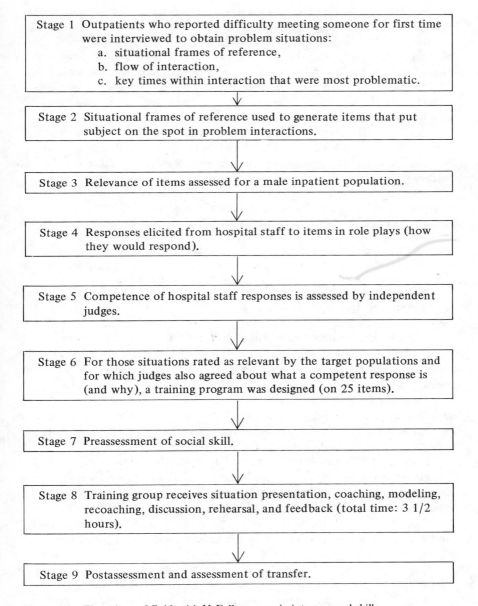

Figure 6.2. Flow chart of Goldsmith-McFall program in interpersonal skills.

Stage 1.   In the first stage of the training program development, a group of subjects were selected who were willing to talk about interpersonal problems. These subjects were selected from seventy-four outpatients actively involved in psychiatric treatment at Illinois State Psychiatric Hospital. The subjects interviewed did not differ significantly on background variables (sex; race; number of schizophrenic, anxiety, or depressive diagnoses) from those subjects not interviewed. In the interviews, problem situations that involved meeting and talking to people were discussed. Situational frames of reference, flow of interaction, and key times of difficulty within the interactional flow were identified. Situational frames of reference mentioned most frequently were dating, making friends, job interviews, relating to authority, relating to service personnel, interacting with attractive or more intelligent people, and interacting with people whose appearance is different from one's own. Key times within the flow of interaction experienced as most troublesome were those where the task was to initiate or terminate interaction, disclose something personal about oneself, break a silence, respond to rejection, and assert oneself.

Stage 2.   Items were then written designed from situational frames of reference identified as problematic. Key times were arranged to put a subject on the spot. For example,

> Let us suppose you had some guests you didn't know too well over to your house. It's been a good evening but you're very tired and want them to leave so you can go to bed. The trouble is nobody's making a move to leave. Finally there's a pause in the conversation and you feel this is your chance to say something.

Stage 3.   Using audio presentation to control for differences in client reading ability, fifty-five problem situations (the Interpersonal Situation Inventory) were presented to a group of male psychiatric inpatients to assess their relevance for this population.

Stage 4.   Simultaneously, responses to the Interpersonal Situation Inventory were elicited from eight hospital staff members. They were asked to role play what they would do in the fifty-five problem items. Situations varied in the amount of response duplication. Eight responses were elicited for each situation.

Stage 5.   Ten hospital staff members were then selected to judge the appropriateness of the eight responses for the problem situations. The judges were also asked to explain why they chose the responses they did as competent or incompetent.

Stage 6.   For the situations rated as most relevant by the target population and for which there was high interjudge agreement about what a competent response is, a training program was designed.

Stage 7.   The skills of subjects assigned to the training program were assessed prior to training by tape-recording the subjects' responses to problem items.

Stage 8.   Due to space limitations, the training procedure will not be described in detail. For more detail the reader is referred to Goldsmith (1973).

Training consisted of the following steps: situation presentation, coaching, modeling, recoaching with projected consequences, discussion, situation representation and rehearsal, feedback, and stimulus re-presentation, rehearsal, and feedback. Training ended when both the subject and the experimenter agreed that the subject's response met the criteria for effective behavior two times consecutively.

Stage 9.   Subjects were reassessed on problem situations and on situations which had been used during the training (to assess transfer of training to new situations). Ratings of audiotapes (rating blindly) showed high (95 percent) agreement. The training group improved significantly (F = 49.78, df = 2/33, p <0.001) and improved more than either of two control groups used in the study.

Cognitive Restructuring

In numerous examples in the psychotherapy literature, authors have suggested that what a person tells himself about his experience affects his behavior. There has been considerable debate about the relationship between cognitions and behavior and of the role of cognitions in learning processes. For the reader who wishes a definition of "cognition," we suggest Ullmann's general view of cognitions as responses by the person that then serve as stimuli, both discriminative and reinforcing. We shall not review this discussion; instead we refer the reader to Bandura (1969, chapter 9), to Lazarus (1971), to Wilkins (1971) for a discussion of cognitive factors in behavior therapy, and to Gerst (1971) for a discussion of symbolic coding processes in modeling. It is becoming increasingly evident that cognitive factors do affect learning and the transfer of learning. We shall review a few of the techniques that have been used to restructure a client's cognitions for behavioral change. (See also Chapter 10 of this book.)

Didactic information   One of the most obvious, but infrequently used methods of clarifying distorted views is some form of didactic information such as books, lectures, articles, or movies. Often, an appropriate referral to a person knowledgeable about the client's area of ignorance is also useful. Many therapists overlook the fact that some clients behave in maladaptive ways simply because they are unaware of alternatives. Direct instruction may be useful in clarifying misconceptions about sex, birth control, etiology, and implications of certain topics such as cancer, epilepsy, genetics, and child growth and development.

Example: Mrs. Glenda Jones became increasingly anxious when she started experiencing discomfort in her uterus. She immediately decided that she had cancer since both her mother and sister had required operations on the uterus and she assumed that she had inherited the "cancer virus." She was reluctant to go to a doctor because she feared learning the "awful truth." Her therapist informed Glenda that cancer is not really inherited, and that a checkup by a competent gynecologist might reveal a simple explanation for her discomfort.

One week later, Glenda, noticeably relieved, reported that her IUD had been improperly inserted and that her pain had subsided completely.

Perhaps one of the most fruitful applications of didactic information is teaching parents simple principles of operant conditioning and behavior management (Patterson and Guillion, 1968).

Covert reinforcement   Cautela (1970) employed covert reinforcement as a technique to modify both maladaptive avoidance and approach behavior by the use of subvocal reinforcers. In this procedure, the individual is administered a Reinforcement Survey Schedule (Cautela and Kastenbaum, 1967) to get some idea of the kinds of things the client finds reinforcing, be it food, music, drinks, women, games, or whatever. Following this, the client and therapist select a thought that is counter to the distressing thought or feeling he presently experiences. After thinking the thought, the client is instructed to reward himself symbolically by thinking of the reinforcing event. Eventually, the self-defeating thoughts and ideas extinguish since they are not being rewarded, while the adaptive thoughts increase in frequency and eventually lead to behavioral changes.

> *Example:*   A twenty-three-year-old college graduate complained that she was plagued by the idea of time passing. She would become anxious when she felt she was not satisfactorily using her hours but, simultaneously, found it difficult to structure time and subjectively felt that time would either slip by rapidly or drag on slowly. Covert reinforcement was employed as part of the treatment program. The thought ("What is now is everything. The next few hours will take care of themselves.") was reinforced by thoughts of baking bread, tramping through the autumn woods, and listening to Nina Simone records. After just a week of thinking and reinforcing the thought at least ten times daily, the patient reported feeling considerably better. She was able to concentrate on her present activity and refrain from worrying about what to do next—she was involved in each minute of her time completely without berating herself for the past or fearing the future.

Thought stopping   Thought stopping is a technique that is useful in dealing with obsessive and upsetting ruminations and injunctions to behave in a certain manner. It is helpful also as a corrective to the self-defeating ideas that clients often exhibit. Pleasant, positive ideas that are incompatible with anxiety are substituted for the worrisome and unproductive thoughts.

Since clients usually complain that they are unable to cease their upsetting ruminations, the therapist must illustrate that this is not true. He asks the client to think the recurring thought and to signal by raising an index finger when the thought is clearly present. Then without warning, the therapist pounds the table (or makes some other loud noise) and shouts "STOP!" Usually, the client is so startled, he reports that the thought has disappeared. He is instructed to immediately transfer his attention to some preselected positive thought or activity. Practice is given in the office at having the client shout "stop" to himself when thinking the upsetting thought and then, finally, covertly verbalizing the word "stop" at the first sign of the appearance of the thought. With repeated practice, clients can become quite adept at "shutting off" self-defeating thoughts and preoccupations and switching their attention to more positive, rewarding ideas.

Rational-emotive therapy   (See Ellis and Harper, 1961.) Rational psychotherapy takes as a major hypothesis that human emotion is caused and controlled by thinking. The individual experiencing positive emotions is usually saying something to himself like, "This is good." In negative emotions, such as anger or depression, the feeling is caused by some variation of the sentence, "This is terrible." If human emotions are the result of thoughts, then it is possible to control feelings by changing thoughts or internalized sentences with which feelings are created in the first place. Ellis focused on changing the irrational, negativistic, illogical, unrealistic, and neurotic links in patients' internalized self-speech which are responsible for subsequent feelings and behavior. He taught clients how to tell themselves saner and more realistic things about themselves. For example, a frequently employed neurotic belief that people hold is "that it's a dire necessity for an adult to be approved or loved by almost everyone for almost everything he does" and that "it is terrible, horrible, and catastrophic when things are not the way one would like them to be—they should be better than they are." By helping to change these self-defeating beliefs to more rational ones—it is pleasant, but not necessary to be approved, and it is unfortunate when things are not the way one would like them to be, but one should accept the way some things are and stop futile complaining—the client is often successful in feeling less cheated and dissatisfied with the world. The client learns that his difficulties, especially his negative feelings (anger, depression, anxiety, and guilt), are maintained by his own irrational attitudes or illogical fears rather than exclusively from past events or external situations. In this approach, the therapist is quite active. He directs, contradicts, and rejects the self-defeating propaganda and superstitions that the client has learned and encourages, persuades, cajoles, and commands the client to engage in activity counter to his irrational nonsensical beliefs.

Example (fictional): Jim Brown could not study for his upcoming Civil Service exam. Each time he sat down with his books, he began thinking of how catastrophic it would be if he failed the test. He could not get a much-needed pay raise, his wife would harass him (and possibly stop making love with him), his friends would find out and call him a moron. These thoughts made him so tense that he would jump from the desk and begin pacing. His own self-defeating thoughts were preventing him from seeing the situation rationally and, in fact, were leading to the very result he feared. The therapist pointed out that it would *not* be catastrophic if he failed; he could always take the test again. His friends would *not* downgrade him, but would probably be sympathetic. And his wife might be disappointed, but not hostile.

Illogical reasoning   Lazarus (1971) discussed several common problems of illogical thinking that prove dysfunctional for clients. These are

1. *Dichotomous reasoning* is the tendency to see things as necessarily at one extreme or the other (true/false, good/bad, rejection/acceptance).

2. *Overgeneralization* is the tendency to generalize to all cases of an event. (Remember all generalizations are false, including this one.)

3. *Excessive reliance on other people's judgment* is one way to avoid the necessity to reason at all.

4. *Enculturation or oversocialization* is an enslavement to the traditional way of doing things and an inability to view things from another perspective.

Personal constructs   A useful metaphor for understanding a client's unique view of his world was given by Kelly (1955). Everyone can be considered an amateur scientist who categorizes and organizes his experiences and develops his own cognitive system to anticipate future events.

The psychotherapist has several powerful tools for understanding a person's unique system for construing experience:

1. *Ignorance:*   In our discussion of the initial interview we mentioned that one of the most forceful tools the therapist has is to realize and use his own stupidity. For example, the therapist must recognize that he does not necessarily know what a patient means by "anger," and what it means to him to be angry.

Example

Client: Well, I felt angry when he said that.
Therapist: How do you mean "angry"?
Client: Like it was going to explode.
Therapist: What do you mean "it"?
Client: Since I've been a little girl, I've watched myself do things and tried to understand what was happening. Like I was two people—the angry one who tries to destroy everything good that happens to me, and the one who watches it all happening.

This principle may seem contrary to the idea that the therapist needs to be empathic and understand what the client says. That is not necessarily so. What we are recommending is that the therapist use the metaphor that he is a traveler through the client's mind. He is being led on a trip and he needs to find out what the sights are and how they relate to each other. He may have seen similar things that will help him. But he should allow the client to paint his own picture of his world, and here ignorance is a helpful tool.

2. *Constructs:* People organize experiences by putting together those things that seem similar and separating categories of events from other categories that seem different. It is by those two simple operations of combining and discriminating that the therapist can understand the way a person constructs his systematic perceptions of the world.

> *Example:* A forty-year-old, attractive woman was seen in therapy. She described her difficulties with her oldest son, comparing his selfishness to her husband's. She described him as "weak and manipulative." She compared her youngest daughter to herself: innocent, shy, and a loner who does not know how to make friends. She complained of her husband who is a traveling salesman, away from home most of the time. "I really am responsible for the family," she declared. She explained that when she was a child she was also responsible for her younger sisters. She described her efforts to equip her children to deal with what she saw as a hostile world. The therapist began to form the image that she saw herself as a Joan-of-Arc figure, on a horse, in full armor, leading her children to battle with a hostile, dog-eat-dog world. She agreed with the image and said that the problem was that she got no recognition for all her efforts.

The therapist in this example tried to understand the client's reporting of events and the main characters in her life. He tried to understand which events she saw as similar, whether she had ever experienced this kind of thing, whether a person reminded her of someone else, how things, people, and events in her life were similar and different, that is, were categorized into a system.

People are likely to change their construct systems when they are unable to categorize and understand experiences in their life, or when their systems consistently lead to bad predictions. The client may be confused by experiences or continually surprised by events. Constructs are then likely to change by exploring alternative ways of understanding the client's experience. The therapist needs to help the client run up against the limits of his ability to make sense out of his experience. This amounts to changing the construct system "from within." Volume I of George Kelly's *The Psychology of Personal Constructs* will be helpful in understanding the theory of constructive alternatives, or ways of modifying a client's perception of the world.

In an interview the therapist may wish to explore the client's perceptions of his experience by "testing the limits" of his system's ability to construe experience.

The therapist's most useful index of reaching the limits of a client's perception is the client's anxiety.

Helping a client correct and clarify distorted perceptions of the world often results in behavioral change, just as altering behavior frequently has a major impact on cognitive and attitudinal feelings. Psychoanalytic theory is based on the principle that behavioral adaptations come with insight (or new ways of explaining and labeling experiential data). In traditional dynamic approaches, the therapist attempts to develop insight or self-awareness by repeatedly interpreting the verbal, affective, and social responses that the patient reports or demonstrates within the treatment hour. Essentially, insight results in new (not necessarily more accurate) ways of labeling and organizing social situations, events, past and present experiences, and the client's own responses.

Personal problem solving   In some cases the ability to "think through" a personal problem may be achieved by the use of a problem-solving guide. Urban and Ford (1971) listed twelve steps in problem solving.

1. The initial recognition of a difficulty
2. The identification (specification) of the problem
3. Analysis of the problem
4. Summary restatement of the problem
5. Selection of objectives which are to be effected
6. Depiction of the criteria (values) by which solutions will be judged
7. Consideration of possible solutions
8. Testing proposals against criteria
9. Selection of a single final solution
10. Operation planning (how it's to be done and who is to do it)
11. Implementation (actuation) of the solution
12. Subsequent evaluation. (p. 8)

A problem-solving outline following these basic steps was used with some success by Stone (1972) with college students as the major method of self-administered therapeutic intervention.

VII

Resistance

"RESISTANCE" is a word used by the therapist when the client is not meeting the therapist's expectations, or not working in what the therapist considers a goal-directed way. A large variety of behaviors are usually subsumed under the heading "resistance"; for example, missing appointments, long silences during therapy sessions, failure to fulfill homework assignments, changing the topic frequently, blocking, not hearing a therapist's remarks, expressing negative attitudes or criticism toward either the therapist or therapy.

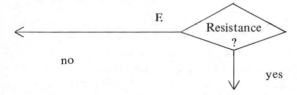

Traditionally, resistance has been regarded as a hypothetical construct, used to *explain* the client's failure to engage in what the therapist considers relevant therapeutic work. Some therapists expect a "resistance phase," which is accompanied by a feeling that work in therapy has stopped. Some therapists interpret this as a reaction to perceived or unconscious threat. Kelly (1955) discussed the term "resistance" in connection with the client's fear of imminent change in the way the client construes his experience. He said that

> The client who exasperates the therapist by his failure to deal with what the therapist wants him to, or by his refusal to see things the way the therapist so clearly sees them, is not necessarily warding off the therapist as a person; more likely he is demonstrating the fact that his construct system does not subsume what the therapist thinks it should. (p. 1101)

Beginning therapists, due to their own frustration, may blame the "resistant patient" for not wanting to change. We feel it would be far better if the therapist reexamined his own expectations. The "bad patient" game may really be a "bad psychotherapy" game.

Goldstein, Heller, and Sechrest (1966) presented an excellent discussion of resistance to behavior change (see Chapter 4). They suggested that:

> ... psychotherapy can be made more effective not only by considering factors responsible for therapeutic success but by paying careful attention to the reasons why psychotherapy is *not* effective. A study of these resistances should help overcome them. (p. 147)

There are likely to be many sources of resistance to behavior change. In the flow chart (Figure 1) we broadly divide the sources of resistance into two categories. We ask the question in decision symbol G:

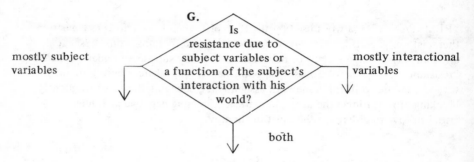

This question is an attempt at a rough dichotomy which involves (1) looking at what the subject brings with him to any situation, that is, his behavioral repertoire (and the conditional probabilities of the occurrence of specific behaviors as a function of the stimulus configurations in the situation) and (2) how the environment responds to the client's behavior.

Resistance may arise because initial psychotherapy efforts have missed complexities in the problem. Todd and Kelley (1972) illustrated this point well:

> The therapist may treat a patient's alcoholism by aversion techniques while ignoring the anxiety for which alcohol is used as a tranquilizer [see *H1*, our flow chart]. The limited repertoire of coping behaviors available to the patient [see *H2*, our flow chart], the pattern of family behaviors which facilitate and reinforce drinking [see *I1* our flow chart], and the set of negative self-responses which discourage the patient from taking corrective action [see *I1*, our flow chart]. (p.7)

You *may* wind up doing all those things, and using all parts of the flow chart (Figure 1). This is an important point. There may not be one secret to unlock the

riddle of the client's resistance to change. There may not be one magical interpretation or insight that does the job. A complex problem may require a set of
interventions to deal effectively with components of the problem.

When the therapeutic program is modified effectively, it may be necessary to
check with the client or client system about the therapeutic contract. We indicate
this on the flow chart by the repeated use of the activity box:

GO TO _D_

On the flow chart (Figure 1) we ask you to "go to _D_" after many activities.
The reason for this is to remind you to check the therapeutic contract again. Things
may have changed. The original presenting problem may suddenly be dropped by
the client for a variety of reasons. For example, parents with a problem child may
suddenly ask for marital therapy after their fear about change is reduced. Although
it may often be a formality, the work involved in returning to _D_ will also often be
rewarded.

VIII

Resistance Due Mostly to Subject Variables

RESISTANCE DUE TO INTERNAL CONFLICT ABOUT CHANGE

THIS PARTICULAR use of the term "resistance" is the one most commonly discussed by dynamic therapists (see Colby, 1951) and by cognitive therapists (see Kelly, 1955). Again, resistance is seen as a change in the client's participation in the therapeutic program. It may be a change in the amount of talk or the quality of the talk; the client may appear to be "stuck" in what he talks about, or struggling from minute to minute to discuss certain issues, or running from important issues, or having trouble keeping appointments. The therapist may feel that change has important cognitive implications which are blocking affective communication in therapy. Perhaps the client is telling himself different things about change that capture him in an approach-avoidance conflict. Dynamic therapists will identify this resistance as a natural phase of psychotherapy which indicates that the therapist has finally met the client's defenses. This is sometimes taken as the signal for work to begin.

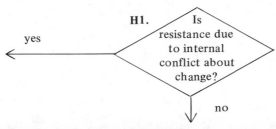

The tools for dealing with internal conflicts involve (1) exploring the client's perceptions and feelings, cognitive restructing (see Section E), and (2) using "interpretations" (See Section H11, Chapter 10).

RESISTANCE DUE TO A SKILL DEFICIENCY

Initial psychotherapy change efforts may have assumed that the client was proficient in certain "good client" role behaviors, and that assumption may have been false. In this instance we are assuming that the client would be perfectly willing to be a "good client" if only he knew how.

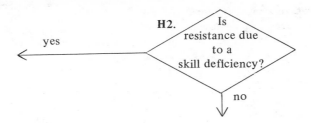

Many psychotherapies which "screen" patients for treatment (for example, psychoanalytic therapy) attempt to assess precisely the question asked by box *H2* when they want to know if the client would be a good potential prospect (for example, is the client "analyzable"?).

Psychotherapy with children was initially deemed difficult if not impossible because children "do not free associate." Play was suggested as a substitute modality for the child's expressions. Play was assumed to be at times symbolic of unconscious thought processes. It was a recommendation that soon became popular, and it is consistent with the Goldstein, Heller, and Sechrest (1966) hypothesis:

> Psychotherapy with resistant patients should be oriented toward accepting and utilizing the role behaviors in which the patients are already proficient.

However, that is certainly not the only alternative. One of the authors has had experience at the University of Colorado Medical Center's psychoeducational facility, the Day Care Center. This facility utilizes Redl and Wineman's (1957) *life-space interviewing* procedure with children. In this program, children (ages five to twelve) are interviewed when they are disrupting their own learning or the learning of other children. The central purpose of this part of the Day Care program is to teach the children to monitor their own behavior, to be able to anticipate its consequences, and to realize the decisions they are in fact making. The staff of the Day Care Center found that when graduates of the program return to the public schools they are reported to be far more capable than most children at "understanding" and "introspecting," and are reported to be easier to work with in discussing problems with public school staff. In effect, this program teaches children "good client" behaviors. It would be a mistake to expect these behaviors from children as a matter of course. Furthermore, it is important to recognize the therapist's role as a teacher.

Example

> Therapist: Dick, why did you do that to the teacher?
>
> Dick: She was making me mad, picking on me. Why doesn't she pick on the other kids?
>
> Therapist: I thought you liked her and were getting along well with her.
>
> Dick: I was, but not any more.
>
> Therapist: Seems to me you get kind of scared by getting along so well with an adult. That's part of your game. When things go well for you, you get worried you're going to get kicked out. Like at home with your parents. So you get control by being such a rotten kid no one can like you. At least then you know what to expect.

This excerpt involved a lecturette by the therapist who suggested that the problem Dick is having with his teacher related to issues the therapist knew were occurring in Dick's family therapy sessions (with another therapist). Part of the life-space interview training has the immediate objective of returning the child to the classroom ready for work.

Psychotherapy with some families may also involve training in behaviors which facilitate good communication. An example of this is training in listening or training in "clean fighting" (Bach and Wyden, 1968).

If the client is not meeting the therapist's expectations of "good client" behavior, then the therapist has two alternatives. He can change his expectations, or he can design a training program. It may not be at all unreasonable to change expectations. For example, some people have a learning history that has caused them to avoid dependent relationships or close affiliations and others have poor verbal introspective ability. Goldstein, Heller, and Sechrest (1966) report research with delinquents which illustrates a change in the usual therapeutic expectations of the "good client" role:

> Others working with aggressive delinquents have gone even further in their de-emphasis of a close relationship. Schwitzgebel and Schwitzgebel (1961), Slack (1960), and Stollak and Guerney (1964) all report procedures in which there is little initial relationship. For example, in the study by Stollak and Guerney, the subject was requested to talk into a tape recorder in a room by himself. The only contact with the experimenter was the minimal interchange that occurred before and after the recording sessions when the subject was being led back to his ward. Subjects were inmates in a diagnostic center for juvenile delinquents. It is interesting to note that a positive relationship with the experimenter did form, but with the subject determining the pace of its development. Every subject talked into the tape recorder as if he were talking to the experimenter, often referring to him by name. Whenever the experi-

menter walked through the ward, most of the subjects would seek him out and exchange a greeting, asking him when the next experimental session would occur. Since their work is still in its preliminary stages, Stollak and Guerney do not report whether this experience had any effect on patient symptomatology. However, Schwitzgebel and Kolb (1964) reporting on a followup of patients participating in "experimenter-subject" psychotherapy, which also involved delinquents talking into a tape recorder, found that after three years subjects in the experiment showed a significant reduction in the frequency and severity of crime when compared with a matched-control group. In both the Stollak and Guerney and the Schwitzgebel and Kolb studies positive relationships with the experimenter did develop, but the relationship was not forced by the experimenter, nor was the ability to form a relationship a precondition for treatment. Sechrest and Strowig (1962) note that teaching machines can have similar advantages in a classroom setting. They suggest that students recalcitrant to normal teacher instruction, might not have their antagonisms toward education aroused to the same degree by an impersonal, non-authoritarian figure such as a teaching machine. (pp. 160–161)

McFall and Marston (1970) demonstrated the efficiency and effectiveness of a semiautomated procedure for training in assertiveness. This program was discussed earlier in this book. It may at times be absurd for the therapist to expect the client whose problem involves relationships with people to solve his problems by first building a real relationship (or a transference neurosis) with the therapist.

If the therapist does decide on a training program, this must be carefully planned. (See Chapter 11 of this book.)

IX

Resistance Due Mostly to Interactional Variables

FREQUENTLY, DYSFUNCTIONAL or symptomatic behavior pays off for the client through immediate gratification, attention from significant others, or its control value. For example, juveniles continue to break the law, despite the threat of reform school or imprisonment. The admiration they receive from others in their peer culture sustains their behavior. Haley (1963 p. 15) suggested that the "crucial aspect of a symptom is the advantage it gives the patient in gaining control of what is to happen in a relationship with someone else." Symptoms may be subjectively distressful, but they may produce a certain degree of consistency and control over others in an otherwise unpredicatable world. Haley gave the example of a patient with an alcoholic wife. Although the patient enjoyed having his own way, his wife always won by getting drunk. The couple could not go out because the wife might drink; the husband could not upset or criticize his wife because she might drink; he could not leave her alone since she might hurt herself when drunk. It may be humilitating to be a drunkard, but the wife was in charge of her symptoms and could use them to control her environment.

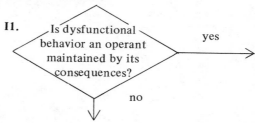

11. Is dysfunctional behavior an operant maintained by its consequences? — yes →

no ↓

Another example of symptomatic behavior paying off is a couple in which the wife's fear of cancer led her to frequent "panics." She would sit and feel her body for tumors. During these panics the therapist discovered that she would call for her husband to "distract" her from ruminating about death. Her husband resented what he described as her "irrational loss of control" and would usually respond by fighting with her. She said, "Even a fight will pull me out of a panic." The panic could be viewed as an operant to obtain attention from her husband. This view is an alternative to exploring the "dynamics" of her own fear of death (which this particular client had already done in psychoanalysis).

In some client systems there are norms that operate to resist change. In this case the dysfunctional behavior may seem to have negative consequences, but the consequences of change are far more negative.

> *Example*:   A fourteen-year-old boy's frequent mischief and trouble with the police were the focus of most of his parents' quarrels. When initial change efforts resulted in an amelioration of the boy's behavior problems, the home situation deteriorated. His mother locked herself in her room and went into a state of deep depression. This situation was so painful to the boy that he ran away from home and was again in trouble with the police. The trouble brought his mother out of her depression and the old family quarrels began anew.

The system behaves as if there is a "negative homeostat" that operates to keep the situation in an intolerable but predictable state. This is an essential point. Dysfunctional behavior can be fruitfully viewed from a systems point of view. The working hypothesis is that the system resists change *as if* it views change as "out of the frying pan into the fire." Systems often operate as if they want only more of what they already have (see Chapter 12).

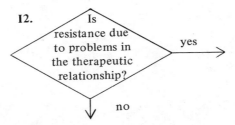

12.   Is resistance due to problems in the therapeutic relationship?   yes

no

At times the "system" which needs to be studied may be the therapeutic interactional system itself. Psychotherapy can be conceptualized as a social influence process. In this conceptualization, resistance to behavior change may be a function of the properties of the therapist, the client, the communication, and the rules established in the relationship.

Resistance within the communication model may also result from the client dealing with issues of *acceptance, affection,* and *control.* The therapist may think of the client's asking questions like: Am I *in* or *out* with this therapist?" "Does he like me?" "Am I important to him?" "Who is in control here?" "Does he think he is an authority figure?" "Who has more or less status in this relationship?"

Schutz (1967) presented an interesting discussion of the importance of the issues of *inclusion, affection,* and *control* as stages of group process in sensitivity training. Haley (1963) discussed control in the therapeutic relationship in individual and family psychotherapy using the relationship between hypnotist and subject as an analogue.

The patient's "yes but" behavior may be related to an acceptance or control issue in the therapeutic relationship. The therapist needs to discuss the "transference," that is, ask "Who am I to this patient at this time? An authority figure? His mother? A lover? A friend?"

It may be the case that the client is responding to the therapist *as if* he represented someone else (transference); conversely, the therapist may be responding to the client *as if* he represented someone else (countertransference). It is important for the therapist to use his feelings and reactions as valuable data in therapy. We discuss issues related to the therapeutic relationship in Section I21 (see Chapter 13).

X

Internal Conflict Intervention

HII. Implement conflict reduction intervention.

INTERNAL CONFLICT may be due to many things and if observed should be explored with the client. In these cases the client is caught in an approach-avoidance conflict. He is approaching change since he has negotiated a therapeutic contract. He is avoiding change because of negative or frightening implications of certain internal mediating thoughts or feelings he associates with change. Here are some examples of what this conflict may be related to:

1. A specific change the client perceives may come about which involves risking the loss of a reinforcer or secondary gain.

   Example: A client became conflicted about becoming more assertive because she feared her boyfriend would like her less.

2. A specific expected loss. For example, a developed sense of independence in an adolescent may lead to fear of leaving home and losing parental love and protection.
3. A general fear of the unknown.
4. The previous learning history of the client which may have linked change of any kind with punishment.

Example (fictional): A six-year-old child cried bitterly whenever his new stepmother and father went out and he was left with a babysitter. This was related to the recent sickness and death of his natural mother which had necessitated frequent and long absences of his father from the home, and then the traumatic loss of his mother.

5. Internal mediating thoughts which imply a redefinition of the patient's core construct of himself.

Example (fictional): Mr. Avis was concerned that any show of sympathy or permissiveness he exhibited with his wife and children would be interpreted as weakness and would cause them to see him as a "pushover." He liked viewing himself as a strong father, unlike the "emasculated" man he saw his father as.

It is good for the therapist to remember that any change in one's life is often accompanied by fear or depression. This is true of changes for the better such as promotion in a job, a move to a more stimulating city, the birth of a long-awaited child. For many people, known discomfort is preferable to uncertain change. Therefore, it is understandable for the client to express worry regarding change and to be reluctant to experiment with new ways of behaving. Several interventions may serve to encourage the client and reduce conflict.

1. Explore in some detail the client's fantasies, expectations, hopes, and fears regarding the results of therapy. Does he think he will become dependent, overly introspective, that he will alienate old friends and acquaintances with his "new self"? Encourage the client to be explicit about the probable effects of treatment and correct any misperceptions.

2. Reassure the client that his fears are not weird, that his doubts and anxieties about whether the new behavior will pay off are natural. The only way of discovering if his fears are valid or not is by experimenting with change (even minor modifications of old routines).

3. Encourage the client to rehearse new responses in your office before attempting them in his natural environment.

Example: Bill Masters, a twenty-four-year-old graduate student, was becoming increasingly depressed about his difficulty with women. He found himself at a loss for words at the mere sight of a coed, though he was able to converse fluently and knowledgeably with older, married women. The therapist suggested that he role play conversations with girls; the first assignment was to practice asking a girl in his statistics class out for coffee. After rehearsing the scene five times, with modifications, corrections, and feedback from the therapist, Bill felt confident enough to try it out the following day.

At the following session, Bill was mildly depressed. Although he *had* conducted himself moderately well and was pleased with his own performance, the girl refused him anyway. Repeated practice over a period of weeks eventually resulted in Bill's securing a date with a secretary in the English department.

4. Begin with minimal changes at which the client is likely to succeed. Program small step-size tasks of increasing difficulty, always taking small enough steps so that failure rarely occurs.

If, for example, a client is terribly shy about meeting people, have him practice simply smiling and saying "Hi!" to individuals he sees everyday. Eventually, incremental steps of greater difficulty can be added—but not steps large enough to generate excessive anxiety.

5. In cases where anxiety is severe, systematic desensitization may be employed. With the patient, construct a hierarchy of all the feared consequences of treatment, arranging them from the least to most feared. After training the client in relaxation, present the steps to the client, one at a time, until anxiety is no longer elicited by the thought of the consequences.

6. Conflict regarding change may be conceptualized as an approach-avoidance conflict where avoidance is greater than approach. To initiate change, one can either reduce avoidance or increase approach.

7. If, after several unfilled promises to attempt agreed-upon tasks, the client is still reluctant, some therapists will pose an ultimatum: No further session until some attempt is made to fulfill the therapy agreement. Alternatively, the client will be charged more for hours when he failed to do his "homework" or be given a shorter session. These interventions are not punishment. Rather they serve to demonstrate to the client the therapist's concern and unwillingness to have him waste his time and money. Before employing aversive contingencies, the therapist must be certain that he understands the nature and rationale of the client's resistance. Care must be exercised in using ultimatums. It is possible that their use will induce a selection bias so that clients are selected to meet the treatment methods currently available.

The most commonly used conceptualization of internal conflict about change is that the conflict represents the client's defenses for coping with threat. Insight-oriented therapists will explore the implications of the problem and change to the client, interpret defenses, and facilitate insights. This activity of the therapist is perhaps the most difficult one to conceptualize in a systematic fashion.

An excellent framework for conceptualizing the process of psychological interpretation (both in assessment and therapy) will be found in Levy (1963). We recommend it as an exciting and stimulating work. Perhaps no other aspect of psychotherapy has been surrounded by as much mystery and mysticism as the subject of interpretation. Levy's book places the phenomenon (and how to make interpretations) on a solid scientific footing. An interpretation is generated by an observation of a discrepancy. The therapist then generates an hypothesis to account for the discrepancy. The therapist views behavior as a sign or symbol of something else in generating an hypothesis. The hypothesis is subject to testing by observing the effect of the statement on the client's behavior both in and outside the therapy hour. An interpretation is often a statement made or question asked by the therapist which focuses the client's attention on his behavior.

A useful working hypothesis for the clinician generating interpretations is provided by Sherlock Holmes. When Holmes met Watson in *A Study in Scarlet*, the first words exchanged were:

> "Dr. Watson, Mr. Sherlock Holmes," said Stanford, introducing us.
> "How are you?" he said cordially, gripping my hand with a strength for which I should hardly have given him credit. "You have been in Afghanistan, I perceive."
> "How on earth did you know that?" I asked in astonishment.
> "Never mind," said he, chuckling to himself. (p. 7)

Later, Sherlock Holmes explains his Afghanistan deduction as part of his "science of deduction." Holmes says,

> From a drop of water a logician could infer the possibility of an Altantic or a Niagara without having seen or heard of one or the other. So all life is a great chain, the nature of which is known whenever we are shown a single link of it. Like all other arts the Science of Deduction and Analysis is one which can only be acquired by long and patient study, nor is life long enough to allow any mortal to attain the highest possible perfection in it. Before turning to those moral and mental aspects of the matter which present the greatest difficulties, let the enquirer begin by mastering more elementary problems. Let him on meeting a fellow mortal, learn at a glance to distinguish the history of the man, and the trade or profession to which he belongs. Puerile as such an exercise may seem, it sharpens the faculties of observation, and teaches one where to look and what to look for. By a man's fingernails, by his coat-sleeve, by his boot, by his trouser knees, by the callosities of his forefinger and thumb, by his expression, by his shirt-cuffs—by *each* of these things a man's calling is plainly revealed. That all united should fail to enlighten the competent enquirer in any case is almost inconceivable. (p. 16)

Dr. Watson is incredulous. He replies, "What ineffable twaddle." Holmes explains to Watson how he knew upon first glance that Watson had been in Afghanistan, how simply in fact that deduction was made (see *A Study in Scarlet*, Doyle, 1890, p. 18).

In many instances the therapist would do well to take Holmes' science of deduction as a useful working assumption for generating hypotheses in psychological interpretation. An experienced clinician once said, "The first ten minutes of any therapy session is like an overture to an opera. All the major themes to be developed later are there in the first few moments of the hour—how the client carries himself, what he says and does, and what he doesn't say or do."

We offer some typical examples of interpretations and the processes by which they are made. These are procedures for generating hypotheses.

1. The therapist suggests a causal connection between two events.

Example
    Client: I don't know why she makes me so angry.
    Therapist: Perhaps your anger toward her is related to your anger toward your mother.

2. The therapist suggests a unifying theme from apparently diverse material and summarizes.

Example
    Client: I don't want to get to know him better. I know I will be disillusioned.
    Therapist: Every time you start getting close to a man, you look for things you don't like about him, wind up disillusioned and break up. What is it about being close to someone that you are avoiding?
    Client: I'm afraid if someone really gets to know me they will see my flaws and want to leave.

3. The therapist suggests a comparison between two events.

Example
    Client: I can't stand him at all. He thinks he's so smart. He's just the *bus driver* in this school.
    Therapist: Wasn't that the way you felt about the gym teacher?
    Client: Yes. Neither of them are "real" teachers.

4. The therapist suggests a contrast between two events.

Example
    Therapist: You say you're a submissive woman, but yesterday you told your minister you would not sing in the choir.
    Client: Yes, but that's easy. I can't do it with men who are, well, sexy.

5. The therapist points out the wish-component of the client's conflict.

Example
    Client: I don't want him to take the bus all the way across town by himself.
    Therapist: Sometimes you would like your son to need you forever even though you want him to be independent, too.

6. A common problem is the client's silence. Sometimes this can be dealt with easily by asking the client what he is thinking about. At times the client plays the "you get it out of me" game. The therapist can say, "Try to think about what is bothering you," and then wait. He may add, "I know it can be hard to get started, but try your best."
    7. The therapist confronts the client with a typical behavior pattern in the interview.

Example
    Therapist: Do you know that every time we talk about your father you ask what time it is and then can't think of what to say?
    Client: I don't want to talk about him. He is dead.
    Therapist: You may want to think of him as dead but he is very much alive.

In all these cases the behavior is taken as a *sign* or *symbol* of something else.
    Interpretations should be made in everyday language: Do not use technical jargon or labels (for example, do not tell a patient he is a masochist). Interpretations are also best when they are only slightly above the client's head, that is, when he is ready to come to an understanding and your comment gives him just the right nudge to it. If you interpret too early in the exploration of a problem, the client will often simply "not hear you" or not understand what you are driving at. If the client is still eager to hold on to his own conceptualization of an event, he will reject your interpretation without considering it. Often, it is necessary to repeat interpretations several times in several different ways, before a client is ready to make it his own. It is not uncommon for a client suddenly to announce, with surprise, "I just understood why I do that," when the therapist has been suggesting the same explanation for the past four sessions! But remember, it is all right to be wrong; you do not have to be right—just be stimulating.

XI

Performance Discrepancy Intervention

H21. Implement performance discrepancy intervention.

IF THE THERAPIST does decide on a training program, he will need to begin by designing one. Any training program must consider the following components:

1. *Behavioral objectives*: These are objectives which unambiguously specify what the patient will be able to do that he cannot do now, the *conditions* (situations) in which he will exhibit these behaviors, and the extent to which he will be expected to exhibit them (*criterion level*).

2. *Step Size*: It is essential that training proceed in increments that are not too large. Often it is more useful to drop back to an easier task than to keep working on the task of higher difficulty. In this way the therapist can program success into the training. For example, in a dating training program, a therapist may have the client speak on the telephone as a step preceding a face-to-face conversation.

3. *Pacing*: It is essential that the pace at which the client moves through the training program be determined by success and essentially by negotiation with the therapist. Artificially determined nonnegotiable deadlines may be deleterious to learning.

4. *Practice*: It is important that the client practice the behaviors and that the practice be distributed over time and over a wide variety of stimulus conditions.

5. *Feedback*: It is important that the client receive feedback, that is, that he receive payoff for his successes and specific corrective suggestions on his failures. Feedback is best if it is immediate, and if it is asked for. The eventual goal in feedback is to have the client be able to proofread his own behavior.

6. *Rehearsal*: The *transfer of training* may be facilitated by rehearsal especially if it is performed in a wide variety of stimulus conditions. Behavior rehearsal or role playing may facilitate transfer.

7. *Task analysis*: Breaking the terminal behavior into its component parts and prerequisite subskills may be helped by task analysis.

Section E on response acquisition discussed some of these concepts. One procedure that is used all too infrequently is

8. Studying the performance of people who competently handle situations that are problematic for the client.

The therapist may be working with a male homosexual whose goals involve establishing lasting relationships with other men. He may do well to interview homosexuals who are competent in situations which are problematic to his client. These interviews may form a basis for a programmatic intervention. Working with a child who is a social isolate in a classroom, the therapist may do well to study what competent performance in making friends is like at that age in that classroom. In marital therapy, the therapist may wish to study the strategies used in problematic situations by couples who feel their marriages are satisfying.

The training program can often begin with a specifically negotiated written contract. For more about training programs and their design, see Espich and Williams (1967), Rowntree (1966), Wolpe and Lazarus (1966), Malott (1972), and Masters and Johnson (1970).

Earlier in this text we suggested that skills could be trained (once the therapist defined the dimensions of a competent response) by repeated presentation of problematic situations and the use of feedback, coaching, and behavior rehearsal. Let us use a therapeutic experience of McFall's (personal communication) as an exercise in designing response acquisition interventions.

> *Exercise*: Let us suppose that you were working with a group of depressed college-age males who consistently resisted implementing homework assignments that involved meeting girls. After several group meetings one of the group members said, "Well, I just don't know what to do," and the rest agreed. Some people said that they could handle some situations and not others. You consider this to be a skill deficiency, and decide to implement a performance discrepancy intervention.
> Design the intervention. Try it before reading any further.

The exercise is difficult, but remember the steps you need to go through. First you must list the problematic situations. Then you must define and describe competent behavior in those situations. Suppose you obtain the following list of problem situations from the group:

1. How to meet a girl
2. Calling for a date
3. What to say when meeting a girl on the way to class
4. Making conversation at lunch in the cafeteria
5. Making conversation at parties or mixers
6. Making conversation on a date
7. When to initiate physical contact (for example, when to kiss)

See if the list will help. What you need to do is think about what the dimensions of a competent response are in those situations.

Example: Here is what McFall did with a small group of four male college students who identified "girl-shyness" as a problem for them.

First , he built a model of effective interaction. He said that there are three stages of interaction: (1) *Permission to enter the personal space*. (For example: greeting. This response would vary as a function of the social situation. In a crowded cafeteria asking someone if you can sit at her table is a different response than doing the same thing in an empty cafeteria.) In this stage the subject explicitly or implicitly states the intention of the inter-action. This usually involves teaching the subject simple things such as saying "excuse me" and waiting until he gets eye contact and a recognition response. (2) Middle stage: *Maneuvering in the personal space* involves the subject's carrying through the intention to socialize. This stage involves some clinical skills learned in a good interviewing course: How to ask a question; how to get someone to open up and talk about himself; asking how a person feels about an area. McFall had subjects practice this skill with strangers (in a restaurant for example) then come back and talk about how it went. (3) Finally, *the leave taking*: This is kind of tough but McFall again stressed the ritualistic aspects of this stage. You do not leave any questions in the person's mind as to *why* you are leaving. McFall set up situations generated by the group members. The group analyzed these situations in terms of what is required in these situations.

The structure of the group meetings was:

> Sessions 1–3 involved staging simple interactions, role playing, and then rehearsing how to behave. Homework was assigned after each session. The first assignment was to go through only the first phase of interaction. This took the pressure off the shy subject who is afraid of failure somewhere down the line of interaction. It was similar to Masters and Johnson's sensitization sessions where they instruct subjects to pet but not to have intercourse.
>
> They brought in girls the second session, one girl for each guy. Instructions were "to get to know the girl." The girls were instructed

to "let the guys carry the ball, to be sympathetic and supportive, and not to cut the guys off."

The third session's assignment was to go to a live setting (library, lounge, cafeteria, bus) which was not set up, to go into it, try the skills, and talk about it in group later on.

Session 4 dealt with sex-related issues. These were mainly raised by the guys. "How do you know when to kiss a girl? Or when to go to bed with her?" An interesting anecdote concerned a man who kept getting rejected early because he was always at the "going to bed" phase without any application of skills at previous phases involving getting to know the girl.

XII

Ecology Modification

Ill. Implement ecology modification intervention.

WHEN DYSFUNCTIONAL BEHAVIOR is maintained by its reinforcing consequences, it is necessary to:

1. Alter the discriminative stimuli that mark the occurrence of the dysfunctional behavior.
2. Change the consequences of the behavior so they become nonrewarding or negative, rather than positive (see Section E for detail).
3. Teach an adaptive means of achieving the same pleasurable consequences, or finding an alternative source of reward.

Example (fictional):   Belinda Thompson, a single twenty-four-year-old secretary who lived alone had been experiencing frightening heart palpitations and fainting spells which her doctor diagnosed as psychosomatic. In therapy, she related exceptionally well to her therapist and, in fact, called him whenever she felt the onset of one of her "attacks." Careful inquiry revealed that Belinda spent the evenings after work alone in her apartment with little to do to occupy her time. At work, where she primarily had her fainting spells, people responded with increased attention and solicitude. Even Belinda's boss became more gentle with her and would inquire about her health. Moreover, Belinda revealed that she enjoyed calling the therapist when she felt alone and anxious about her future.

Belinda's attacks were set off by feeling "overwhelmed with work" or being alone and lonely. The attacks were reinforced by reduced work pressure and increased attention from others. The therapist also reinforced Belinda's symptoms. The therapist therefore told Belinda that time with him could only be obtained in certain ways. She was assigned interpersonal homework each week (for example, joining a book discussion club, calling up a friend to go shopping, planning a weekend trip, or inviting someone over for dinner). Calling the therapist to report an attack would result in a loss of 10 minutes of therapy time. A further condition was that each week Belinda had no attacks (which she tracked), there would be a reduction of $5 on the cost of her therapy hour that week. Belinda's attacks rapidly ceased. She reported increased pleasure from social contacts and discovered ways other than fainting to deal with her boss's demands.

Haley (1963) suggested a number of ways of gaining the cooperation of a patient who is reluctant to relinquish his symptoms. For example, he described an approach in which the therapist urged the patient to continue displaying the symptoms but with some small modification. The patient suffered from hysterical choking and gagging that occurred before bedtime. Once the patient felt comfortable that the therapist was not going to take away her inhibitions, he used her fears to produce change. He accepted the patient's notion that she must undress in the dark in a room other than her bedroom so that her husband could not see her. He then suggested that the patient "spontaneously" think of dancing into the bedroom in the dark when her husband could not see her. She felt she could do this in an uninhibited way since the room was totally dark and no one could observe her. When she did this, the patient went to bed giggling. Since she could not giggle and gag and choke at the same time, the symptoms diminished and she was then able to learn new ways of dealing with her husband.

Haley suggested making a specific contract with the patient. He suggested to the patient that if he really wanted to change his behavior, he would faithfully follow the therapist's instructions for a few days. A program was then prescribed in which the symptomatic behavior was positively reinforced but was met with negative consequences. For example, in the case of a man who said he could sleep only two hours each night, Haley instructed the man to scrub and wax the floors in his apartment at bedtime and throughout the night for the next four nights. The patient detested the chore since he hated the smell and feel of wax. The patient complied the first night and the second. By the third evening, he thought he would rest for just a while and then complete the assignment, but slept soundly throughout the night. The fourth night and thereafter the same thing happened. The mere thought of waxing the floor instead of sleeping was a powerful incentive to successful sleep.

Haley also suggested encouragement (and at times exaggeration) of the symptom but at the control of the therapist. For example, encouraging a fight-shy couple not to fight but simply rehearse in their minds what they would like to say to their spouse, instructing a wife who always nags her husband to nag him regularly for three hours each evening, and so on. According to Haley (1963, p. 147), "This procedure not only gives the therapist some control of what the couple is doing and lays the groundwork for a later shift, but it also utilizes whatever rebellious forces are latent within the couple."

A functional analysis in which antecedents, dysfunctional behavior, and consequences (ABC analysis) are carefully charted often leads to hypotheses for interventions. The therapist is able to determine if the response to be altered is one that invariably produces positive consequences (and what these are), *who* the significant people are in maintaining the response, where and when the response typically occurs, as well as other data that might otherwise be overlooked. A few summary principles of contingency management may be helpful in changing the ecology. First, *be consistent*. It is important not to make rules that are lax in application. Second, *think small*. Small steps in the design of objectives are best. Third, *establish functional behavior*. That is, build in behaviors that are likely to be reinforcing for the client in a variety of behavior settings. Fourth, start with those behaviors that are in the *client's response repertoire*. Fifth, only a *trial and error* process will be effective. Stick with it; if at first the ecology modification is unsuccessful, recycle and redesign it. (See Malott, 1972, for examples.) If at first you don't succeed, re-evaluate, intervene, and evaluate again.

XIII

Resistance as a Function of Therapeutic Communication

121. Implement therapeutic communication intervention.

RESISTANCE AND THE THERAPEUTIC RELATIONSHIP

GOLDSTEIN, HELLER, AND SECHREST (1966) discussed the varieties of resistance to behavior change in psychotherapy according to a communication model proposed independently by Hartley and Hartley (1952) and Cohen (1964). In this model communication is considered a process of social influence. Breakdowns in communication occur as a function of the nature of the communicator, the communicant, or the communique. After reviewing the literature, Goldstein, Heller, and Sechrest suggested hypotheses which can be tested in the psychotherapy setting. We offer some of their hypotheses as useful considerations for the therapist.

    1. Psychotherapy with resistant patients should be oriented toward accepting and utilizing the role behaviors in which the patients are already proficient.

    This suggests that for some patients the therapist needs to consider other means of treatment that may not require the formation of a close interpersonal and verbal communication. The patient may respond to action orientation or greater structure rather than the unconditional permissiveness of many forms of therapy.

    2. Impersonal and machine therapies are recommended initially for those patients who are avoidant of close interpersonal relationships.

    3. Action therapies are recommended initially for patients unpracticed in introspection.

    4. Resistance in psychotherapy is reduced as the threat value of therapeutic communications is reduced.

5. Unambiguous messages decrease the threat value of therapeutic communications.

6. Messages that encourage delayed compliance decrease the threat value of therapeutic communications.

7. Resistance in psychotherapy can be reduced by training the patient to view the therapist as a positive but discriminating reinforcer (rather than an unconditionally positive reinforcer).

8. Resistance in psychotherapy can be reduced by maximizing the opportunities for imitation learning by the patient.

It may also be the case that the client is responding to the therapist *as if* he were someone else, and endowing him and the relationship with the characteristics of another person (or persons) and his relationship with him (or them). This phenomenon is sometimes called "transference." It is not a mystical pheonomenon, though it may be surprising and quite intense when it occurs. Using a learning framework, transference may be conceptualized in terms of stimulus and response generalization.

TRANSFERENCE: THE CLIENT'S REACTIONS TO THE THERAPIST

Transference means that the client feels toward the therapist the way he did or does toward another significant figure in his life. It is often restricted as a definition to feeling toward the therapist as he did toward important figures in his childhood. The important part of the transference as a resistance is that it is the client who makes the projection and that this projection interferes with the course of treatment in the real therapeutic relationship. The term "acting out in the transference" means that the patient is acting toward the therapist as if he were playing a role in a script written in another chapter of the patient's life. He may be seeing the (male or female) therapist as a rejecting mother, or a powerful mother who gives affection but can withdraw it, or as a powerful authority or father, or as a sibling rival, or an ideal model. The point is that the therapist is being seen *as if* he were another figure who played (or plays) an important part in the client's life.

To work on this resistance it is often useful to talk about it—to ask the client about how he sees the therapist; does the therapist remind him of anyone else in his life in some ways; generally, what does the client feel about his relationship with the therapist; what does he wish the relationship to be like; and what are his fears that the relationship will become?

COUNTERTRANSFERENCE: THE THERAPIST'S REACTIONS TO HIS CLIENTS

Much has been written regarding the patient's tendency, over the course of therapy, to view his therapist in various unrealistic ways (such as an idealized parental figure, as an omnipotent model whom he attempts to imitate, as an authoritarian, as a remote mind reader, and so forth). It is likewise true that the therapist, over time, is likely to experience a variety of emotions and reactions toward his patient, some more realistic than others. These reactions may certainly affect the therapeutic course and merit examination by the conscientious therapist.

For example, a therapist who has difficulty handling his own feelings of anger might tend to inhibit a client's expression of anger. He may change the subject, look disinterested, or underplay the extent of the client's reaction. Conversely, a therapist who leads a rather routine, conventional life may inadvertently reinforce the asocial, sexual acting out of a youthful patient. By overemphasizing certain aspects of the patient's behavior with differential attention or interest, the therapist may lose objectivity and impede client improvement.

Sullivan (1953) wrote, "We are all more human than otherwise." This certainly applies to our behavior as therapists. Despite a desire to be cool, objective, and dispassionate, it is often difficult not to react defensively at the angry accusations of an impatient or dissatisfied client. When an attractive young female patient behaves seductively, a male therapist might become aroused. Furthermore, it is possible that the client, who is alert to the sensitivities of the therapist, may manipulate these "vulnerable spots" to his own advantages, often sabotaging treatment efforts.

Rather than hide his own reactions from the client, the therapist's reactions should be used in therapy as relevant data. If the therapist tells the client about reactions to him, the client is better able to understand others' reactions to his communications and may better monitor his behavior. Acceptance of all a client's behavior without comment is neither realistic in terms of generalization to the extratherapy world nor respectful of the client.

Wolberg (1954, p. 754) suggested that the therapist ask himself the following questions as a means of sensitizing himself to possible problem areas in dealing with a client:

1. How do I feel about the client?
2. Do I anticipate seeing the client?
3. Do I overidentify with or feel sorry for the client?
4. Do I feel any resentment or jealousy toward the client?
5. Do I get extreme pleasure out of seeing the client?
6. Do I feel bored with the client?
7. Am I fearful of the client?
8. Do I want to protect, reject, or punish the client?
9. Am I impressed with the client?

If answers to these questions suggest difficulties to the therapist, he might ask himself why such feelings exist: What is the client doing to stir up such attitudes? What is the therapist bringing to the hour as a result of his own previous experience? By "knowing thyself," you are better able to handle unreasonable and inappropriate reactions and to use nondistorted observations to therapeutic advantage.

If the would-be clinician repeatedly encounters difficulties with all clients, or a specific type of individual (for example, unassertive men), he might question whether his own "hang-ups" are impeding his effectiveness as a therapist. In such cases, the clinician might consider the possibility of obtaining therapy for himself or at least consulting regularly with another more experienced clinician.

One of the basic parts of changing the therapeutic relationship is to give and ask for feedback about the relationship from the client.

XIV

When All Else Fails

J. Return to A, reassess, renegotiate, and so on.

THERE ARE THOSE sad times when something has gone awry. Often key people or settings have been omitted in the problem analysis. There may have been something else lacking in the problem assessment phase. It is not clear why you have arrived at Section J. We suggest that you consider discussing the problem with the client and then return to Section A for a new look at things. You may profit by calling in a colleague as a consultant on the case. You may decide that the case falls outside of your powers, or you may decide to refer the case elsewhere. If both you and the client are willing to continue, we do suggest you return to Section A of the flow chart and, in effect, reopen the case, reassess the problem, renegotiate the contract, and restructure change efforts.

One technique for problem solving that we have found helpful is called *force field analysis*, suggested by Lewin (1938). In this technique we use the following operating assumption: Things are "stuck" because an equilibrium exists between those forces facilitating change and the opposing restraining forces. You can then

1. List facilitating forces for change.
2. List restraining forces resisting change.
3. List alternative intervention strategies which can be obtained by
   a. strengthening facilitating forces
   b. adding new facilitating forces.
   c. weakening or removing restraining forces.
4. List the advantages and disadvantages (including costs) of each intervention strategy.
5. Decide how to evaluate the effectiveness of any intervention at this point of therapy.
6. Intervene, evaluate, and recycle if necessary.

XV

Monitoring Change

K1. Monitor change.

THIS CHAPTER will introduce the time-series design as a way to use the client or client system as its own control. To evaluate the changes over time in the same subject (person, classroom, family), the subject is compared to himself over time. This chapter will suggest two methods for using time-series data to generate hypotheses for interventions. The next chapter will present a method for the statistical assessment of the impact of interventions via time series using a crude but easily applied graphical method called "Shewart Charts." The reader is referred to Gottman (1973) and Glass, Willson, and Gottman (1973) for a more sophisticated discussion of time-series methods. (See also the appendix.)

We propose that graphical methods of monitoring progress toward therapeutic goals will be adequate in most clinical applications. The therapist wants to do three things with data over time:

1. Monitor change
2. Generate hypotheses for intervention
3. Assess the effectiveness of planned interventions.

In monitoring change, data are gathered at critical points to provide feedback before progressing to the next stage of the intervention plan. For example, if the client is learning a social skill, it may be important to assess his mastery of requisite subskills before continuing the social skill acquisition program.

To generate hypotheses for intervention we suggest two methods: (1) the annotated record, and (2) studying concommitant variation.

We think it is unfortunate that the analysis of time-series data is necessarily complex. We hope that the graphical methods we describe will make time-series analysis sufficiently available to the reader. There is, however, no substitute for the simplicity of the computer program printout of simple Student's *t* values which tell the user directly if a change was significant or not. We urge a clinic with any interest in ongoing evaluation to install and use the computer program presented in the appendix of this book.

We hope that as time-series methods become used more often, they will become more accessible in the evaluation of psychotherapy. In the meantime we think that the graphical procedures we suggest will have general utility in most cases.

THE ANNOTATED RECORD

It is useful to combine the keeping of an historical log or journal of events in the client's life with a graph charting such events over time. Hypotheses about change can be generated using this annotated record. For example, in a program for potential high school dropouts, teachers assumed they had made major break-throughs with a student after having a long, emotional, intimate talk. There were three instances of this event. Time-series analysis on three behavioral indicators, however, showed that each of the students significantly avoided the teacher more after the talk, did not improve in academic performance, and significantly increased classroom participation in a disruptive manner (Gottman, 1971). The annotated graph permits one to generate hunches which relate to observed changes in the graph. These hunches may lead to intervention hypotheses.

Example (fictional):   The Annotated Record. A college senior majoring in history complained of being unable to accomplish anything in studying for his final exams. He reported a vague sense of alienation and purposelessness. He said he often became depressed "for no reason at all," and could not change his mood easily. The therapist asked him to keep a journal of his activities, thoughts, and critical events for one week. The senior was told to record these events at least twice daily, and also to score each entry from 0 to 100 depending on how he felt. A score of 50 was considered "neutral," a score of 100 meant "feeling great," and a score of 0 meant feeling "extremely depressed." He was also asked to keep track of his study time.

JOURNAL

Time	Study time	
Time	*Study time*	
Monday A.M.	0	Saw my major professor. He gave me a pep talk about getting through exams. Felt like going to work. Felt great. *Score: 90*

Monday	A.M.	2 hrs.	Tried to study but got horny. Called Eileen, had a good screw but not too good a time after. She's so demanding. Felt like a jerk for not putting in the study time. *Score: 20*
Monday	afternoon	2 hrs.	Cooked dinner. Really stuck to my diet tonight. Had a delicious T-bone. Felt good except about eating alone. *Score: 60*
Monday	evening	0	Decided to go shopping. Bought a new watch with underwater dials and other fancy stuff. A present to myself. Feel fine. *Score: 75*
Tuesday	A.M.	0	Watch doesn't work. It just stopped. I'll have to take it back. Ugh! Hate to deal with salesmen. It's gonna be a bad day. *Score: 30*
Tuesday	P.M.	0	Really got mad at Professor Snavely's comments about my paper. I'd like to kick his butt. Went to the College Inn and had a few beers instead. Crying in my beer. I knew it would be a lousy day. *Score: 15*
Tuesday	evening	0	God! I forgot to take cash out for tonight's date. Now bank is closed. I keep forgetting things. I'm in no mood to see Eileen, I'll tell you that. *Score: 10*
Tuesday	evening	0	Had a great time with Eileen! Sometimes she is so much fun to be with. Looked like a million bucks! It's just nice to be with her sometimes. Went canoeing—very romantic stuff. *Score: 95*
Wednesday	A.M.	1/2 hr.	I'd better return that

			watch today with all its dumb dials. But I've also *got* to study. I'm going to study all day and all night. *Score: 60*
Wednesday A.M.	0		I got carried away with a novel about Prussian international intrigue. Can't put it down. Well, it's vaguely related to quals, I guess. Why didn't I become a novelist. No talent, I suppose. *Score: 40*
Wednesday P.M.	0		Finished the novel! Great! I'm inspired to write one of my own. I'll really do it, by God. I can still study for quals, too! *Score: 80*
Wednesday evening	2 hrs.		Eileen called. Her mother and father are hassling her and she's all depressed. She's *got* to see me. I told her I've got to study for quals. Was she mad! You just can't win. *Score: 20*
Wednesday evening	1/2 hr.		Bob, Tom, Ira came over late (midnight) with a huge bottle of vodka. I *was* studying. Honestly. But you can't say no to a great bunch like them. Got smashed. *Score: 50*
Thursday A.M.	0		Hungover. Whoo! Have an exam today. It'll be easy. I love that class—Professor Pfankuchen's class in International Law. He's interested in how you *think*. A real switch. Oh yes, I'll have to return that damn watch. *Score: 50*
Thursday P.M.	0		That exam was actually fun to take. I think I did well. You know what? Reading that novel helped. Really, it gave me an idea for the essay. What do you know? *Score: 75*

Thursday	P.M.	0	Tried to return that watch. The guy claimed I dropped it. I told him I didn't. That bastard! I ought to smash his window. Went to the College Inn for a few beers. *Score: 30*
Thursday	evening	0	Saw Eileen. She's much better but quite cool to me. And a bit sarcastic. Wow! I apologized so she said, "we'll see." Like I'm being tested or something. I didn't say anything. Everywhere you turn you are getting tested. *Score: 6*
Friday	A.M.	0	Woke up feeling sick. I really blew my diet after that date. I ate everything in the kitchen that wasn't walking or nailed down. I think I had a nightmare about Eileen. She was roasting me on a barbecue spit. That bitch. Today, I've got to write the questions for the introductory history exam. Deadlines! Deadlines! *Score: 30*
Friday	P.M.	0	Saw a lovely creature, a beautiful girl on the bus and decided to go up and talk to her, and say, "I'm your dream man, baby," or something. Kept putting it off. She got off the bus. She was probably my type, too. I felt like a real jerk. Can you believe this? I just bought a three-year life insurance plan. In case I die in the next three years, Eileen gets 10,000 bucks. And I can't afford that. *Score: 20*
Friday	evening	8	There I was studying. I got quite a bit done, too. Studied from about 9 till dawn. That's eight hours (see them down there, *8* hours). Then I saw the sun come up like a big bloodshot eye. Felt tired but good. *Score: 95*

Saturday	P.M.	0	I can't believe it. I just talked to Eileen on the phone for five solid hours. And then I'm going out with her tonight. Guess what I just remembered as I'm writing this—I forgot to do those exam questions. Am I gonna catch hell on Monday. *Score: 40*
Saturday	evening	0	Well we're back together. I had to apologize like mad and swallow a bunch of criticism. Christ, Eileen, what do you do, keep a god-damn *list*? But I suppose it is worth it. When you're horny, you pay. *Score: 20*
Sunday	A.M.	0	Would you believe that Eileen and I went to church. Yes, we did. Now I remember why I quit going. The minister said, "We must all find the Lord inside ourselves." I can't even get my money back for my watch. Maybe if I found the Lord inside me, I could zap that bastard with a bolt of lightning. I thought that was pretty funny, so I told Eileen. She was madder than a hornet for my making fun of the minister, who is "wiser than I'll ever be"! I'm in dutch again. I'm gonna join the Foreign Legion. *Score: 5*
Sunday	P.M.	1 hr.	I was about to do those exam questions, but was feeling low, when Ira called and all he said was "Vodka you son-of-a-bitch." I came over and he, Bob, and Tom were there with vodka and four young ladies. A lovely evening indeed. We got drunk playing monopoly until 6 A.M., then went for breakfast! *Score: 30*

Monday   A.M.

Well, I am about to catch
hell about the exam questions.
Maybe he will give me an
extension. I can do them if
I stay up all night tonight.
I hate getting chewed out.
Hate it.   *Score: 10*

The therapist categorized the journal entries as follows:

Mood: 0–25	*26–50*	*51–75*	*76–100*
1. bad time with girlfriend	1. gets carried away with novel instead of studying	1. sticks to diet	1. pep talk with professor leads him to make plans
2. not studying after he'd planned to	2. gets drunk with boys instead of studying	2. makes plans to study and return the watch	2. plans to write a novel and to study
3. bad feedback on paper from prof.	3. unable to successfully return defective watch	3. does well on exam; enjoys exam	3. has a great time with Eileen
4. forgets to get cash for date	4. forgets to do exam questions	4. studies for 8 hrs. as planned	4. buys himself a present (watch)
5. says no to Eileen	5. gets drunk at party instead of writing exam questions		
6. apologizes to Eileen	6. blow his diet		
7. doesn't approach girl on bus after he had planned to			
8. apologizes to Eileen			
9. Eileen gets mad at his joke about minister			
10. about to get chewed out for not doing exam questions			
11. buys life insurance when he doesn't want to			

He identified the following problem areas:
1. sticking with plans; organizing his day to follow his plans;
2. being able to fight with Eileen instead of dealing with all issues between them by apologizing and feeling depressed later;
3. being assertive; for example, successfully returning watch, saying no when he has made other plans, not buying life insurance he cannot afford.

The annotated record has helped the therapist obtain valuable qualitative, as well as quantitative, information. There is still quite a bit of information the therapist can tap. For example, he can try to discover what kinds of events are associated with the widest mood swings.

Another way the therapist can continually examine a record is to search for variables that appear, at least to some extent, to control the variable of interest. We call this studying "concommitant variation."

STUDYING CONCOMMITANT VARIATION

An interesting example of this process was discussed by Edwards and Cronbach (1966). They received Fisher's (1921) extensive analysis of yield in wheat in bushels per acre. Fisher's analysis has the qualities of a good piece of detective work by Sherlock Holmes, and is a useful example of what the therapist can do when he searches for causal connection between variables. They wrote:

> [Fisher] found that after he controlled variety, and fertilizer, there was considerable variation from year to year. This variation had a slow up and down cycle over a seventy year period. Now Fisher set himself on the trail of the residual variation. First he studied wheat records from other sections to see if they had the trend; they did not. He considered and ruled out rainfall as an explanation. Then he started reading the records of the plots and found weeds a possible factor. He considered the nature of each species of weed and found that the response of specific weed varieties to rainfall and cultivation accounted for much of the cycle. But the large trends were not explained until he showed that the upsurge of weeds after 1875 coincided with a school-attendance act which removed cheap labor from the fields, and that another cycle coincided with the retirement of a superintendent who made weed removal his personal concern. (p. 64)

Economists search for connections between two time series in the hope of finding "lead indicators." A lead indicator is a series whose fluctuations are predictors of the fluctuations of another series; for example, wholesale prices are a lead indicator of retail prices since a rise in wholesale prices will lead to a delayed rise in retail prices (note that a drop in wholesale prices may *not* lead to any effect on retail prices).

If two series vary together it is true that they may not be causally connected. A planned intervention is necessary to ascertain causal connection. Correlation does not imply causation. Of course, if two series are uncorrelated, they will usually not be causally connected. Concommitant variation does not imply causation, but neither does anything else. Causal connection is never demonstrated; rather, we successively eliminate rival hypotheses which militate against confidence in causal connection.

Example: We discussed lead indicators in a brief example in Section C, under problem assessment. However, consider the example of our college senior presented above. If we graph his average daily mood and also graph the amount of daily study time, we can see that there is some degree of concommitant variation. The correlation coefficient is: *r* = 0.64. The therapist might hypothesize that the client's mood is related to the amount of time he studies.

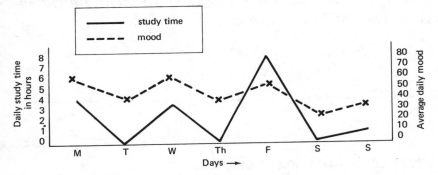

Figure 15.1.   Cross correlation shown in a client's study time and mood.

For a mathematical presentation of the analysis of concommitant variation and lead indicators see Glass, Willson, and Gottman (1973).

XVI

Assessing the Impact of a Planned Intervention

K1. and K2. Intervene when necessary to facilitate change; assess impact of intervention.

SINGLE-SUBJECT EVALUATION OF CHANGE

THE ASSESSMENT of change over time can be made with just one client (or client system) by using repeated measurement over time. Perhaps the most promising design to assess the impact of a planned intervention is the *interrupted time-series design*. In this design, a series of measurements or observations precedes and follows a planned intervention. The observations prior to the intervention are called the "baseline." In the baseline, the movement of the client toward therapy goals is monitored. A planned intervention may be introduced to facilitate change toward stated goals. An example of this design is plotted in Figure 16.1.

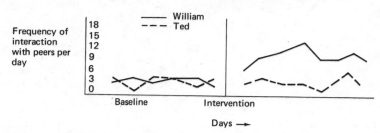

Figure 16.1.   Frequency of a social isolate's interaction with peers.

A shy, eight-year-old boy was referred to the clinic by his teacher. She said that William just seemed "out of it, often staring into space and humming to himself at his seat." The therapist asked the teacher to administer a sociometric scale and William was rated as one of two social isolates in the class. The other isolate was a boy named Ted. None of the other children picked William or Ted as their friend, or as someone they would want to play with, go to for help, or work with on a special project. The therapist enlisted the help of a paraprofessional teacher aide in the school. She counted the frequency of William's and Ted's interactions with peers. They are plotted in Figure 16.1.

The therapist and teacher then designed an intervention. They listed William's skills: He was a good puppeteer, a good artist, and good at mathematics. The teacher formed groups to work on a puppet show and an art display for the library. William was in both groups. The teacher met with these groups and tried to coach William on how to participate, and as unobtrusively as possible reinforced the group for using William's talents. At the same time, the therapist spent three hours a week meeting with groups that included William. He gave the groups decision-making tasks (for example, "Pretend you are planning a party for the class and have to decide what food to get and what to do. You have $10 to spend. Try to agree with each other and discuss your ideas.") During these tasks, the therapist coached the children in listening to each other, summarizing, reinforcing each other's ideas, and managing conflict. William was often the focus of this coaching.

The graph shows that William began increasing the amount of time he interacted with his classmates. The sociometric scale was readministered and showed that three people listed William as someone they would want to work with on a project, and he gained one friend (more about Ted later).

Campbell and Stanley (1963) suggested that the interrupted time-series design is an excellent quasi-experimental design in settings that typically keep archival records over time. Schools, for example, usually keep records about attendance, tardiness, disciplinary incidents, grades, achievement test scores, and teacher comments. Campbell (1969) discussed the use of the interrupted time-series design to evaluate the impact of political or legal reforms. These reforms are usually administered to an entire political unit. For example, a crackdown on speeding may be ordered by the governor of a state in response to high traffic fatalities. This is similar to interventions made in a treatment program with a single client. A clinic, hospital ward, or community mental health center may set up a new policy and use archival data to assess changes. A mental health center may use such data as rates of suicide, divorce, unemployment, child battering, drug arrests, mugging, or a variety of other indexes which may be kept by health and law enforcement agencies as a matter of course.

The time-series design is subject to a major criticism that something else may have happened to the client beside the planned intervention that was responsible for change. This is a valid criticism. To test it, the intervention will have to be replicated, either in treatment or in the laboratory. Gottman, McFall, and Barnett (1969) proposed a design involving at least two subjects for increased power to eliminate rival hypotheses accounting for effects. This design is called the "time-lagged control" design. This design involves intervening with one subject while withholding the intervention from a second subject for a time, and then administering the intervention again to the second subject. For example, the intervention was administered to Ted, the second social isolate in the class. (See Figure 16.2.)

This design provides both an independent replication of the effect and a control during the time the intervention is withheld. The time-lagged control design may also avoid the ethical problem of withholding a treatment from a needy client. Treatment is withheld only for a time and is administered once it has been shown to be effective.

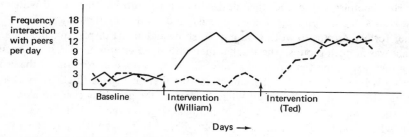

Figure 16.2.   Time-lagged control design.

This design is not new to psychology. Hilgard (1933) presented a time-lagged control study of two twins. This study showed a maturational trend to the data in the baseline period. In the evaluation of psychotherapy this would be equivalent to progress over time toward stated goals (increasing self-concept, decreasing fear, increasing assertiveness, and so on). The figure suggests the temporary effects of intensive training in digit memory over and above maturational trends. The intervention is similar to a therapist intervention to facilitate change.

Chassan (1967) discussed the advantages of time-series designs (which he called "intensive" designs) in the assessment of psychotherapy. Browning and Stover (1971) discussed the use of "same-subject" designs to evaluate the impact of behavior modification with emotionally disturbed children.

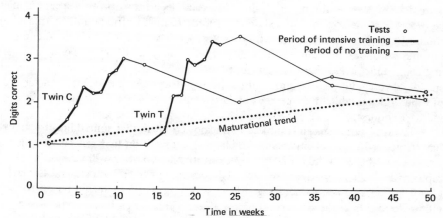

Figure 16.3.   A time-lagged control experiment with identical twins showing effects of intervention beyond maturational trend.

HOW TO ASSESS THE STATISTICAL SIGNIFICANCE OF CHANGE FOLLOWING AN INTERVENTION

The problem of assessing the impact of an intervention with appropriate statistical techniques is not a trivial one. Glass, Willson, and Gottman (1973), Gottman (1973) and Gottman, McFall, and Barnett (1969) discuss this problem in detail. The reader is referred to Glass, Willson, and Gottman (1973) and Kepka (1972) for a thorough statistical presentation of the problem of assessing the impact of an intervention. Let us say here that traditional tests of statistical significance applied to change from preintervention to postintervention period averages are inappropriate. Also, a mere graphical presentation of data (rely on the old "eyeball") is also inappropriate (see Gottman, 1973).

We shall illustrate the point about comparing baseline and postintervention period averages (using the *t* test). In Figure 16.4, the baseline period shows the problem of increasing infant mortality. The *X* marks the average infant mortality rate for the baseline period. Suppose an innoculation program for pregnant mothers was undertaken as the intervention planned to change this dire situation. There were two possible outcomes, illustrated by the dotted and solid lines respectively. In line A, the solid line, we see that the intervention was a failure. There has been no decline in infant mortality—it continues to soar with the same trend as in the baseline. In line B, the dotted line, we see that the intervention was successful, indeed. There has been a reversal of the trend. However, suppose we were merely to examine the *X* for dotted line B (marking the average for that period following the intervention). The *X* for the successful intervention is equal to the *X* for the baseline. We would, if we merely compared averages, say, "An average of 270 infants per 100,000 were dying before you intervened, and an average of 270 were dying during the period following your intervention. Some change!"

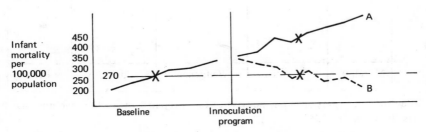

Figure 16.4. Assessment of the effects of an intervention showing the inadequacy of comparing averages before and after intervention.

The analysis of data over time is more difficult because the data are often not statistically *independent*. If data are statistically dependent, then this means we can predict the future by using the past (with some small random error). The fact that most time-series data are statistically dependent introduces some difficulty in statistically analyzing the effect of an intervention.

Again, for a statistical analysis of this problem and a computer program which can be applied to assess the effects of intervening, the reader is referred to the appendix of this book. We will present a graphical answer to this question that is mathematically sound, but less powerful statistically. To teach you this graphical method we will go through several steps. First, we begin with an *assumption*.

Assume that observations over time
are statistically independent.

The procedure we begin with (if that assumption is met) is based on a method for industrial quality control suggested by Shewart (1931). It has also been proposed in the evaluation of educational programs by Gottman and Clasen (1972).

SHEWART CHARTS

The following example is taken from Gottman and Clasen (1972).

Example: A manufacturer of Dr. Denton pajamas must make sure that the heights of the rear flap is the right size [6 inches give or take a small amount of tolerance (1/4")]. To determine whether the production process is in proper working order, a sample of six pajamas is selected every day and the average size of the flap in this sample is computed. Here is our quality control chart:

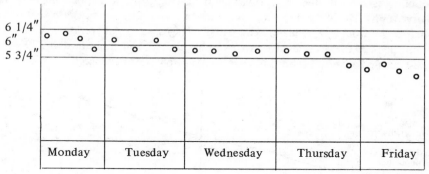

Sometime on Friday it might be wise to call a repairman for the machine that cuts the flaps. (p. 224)

This example illustrates the use of Shewart control charts when:

1. observations are assumed independent, and
2. tolerance limits are known ahead of time.

Until the next section, we will continue to assume our observations are independent. This means that they vary randomly around some constant value. As soon as we get "sufficient" drift away from this constant value, we will know that things have changed. The question is, How do we decide what is "sufficient" drift if we do not set limits the way the pajama manufacturers did? For example, if we are graphing the frequency a child in a classroom hits other children, how can we set tolerance limits? We *can* set a terminal goal, but can we assess change before actually arriving *at* the goal?

The answer is yes. We use the concept of a *standard deviation,* summarized in the following steps:

1. Plot the data for a *baseline period* before intervening. Calculate the mean and standard deviation of the data over this period.

2. Draw a two standard deviation band above and below the mean and keep charting.

3. Intervene, and see if at least two successive observations drift outside the band. If so, there has been a statistically significant shift (which will occur by chance less than 5 times out of 100). These are "rules of thumb" used in industrial quality control charts.

Example:

1. A school psychologist charts fourth-grader Tom Jones' "time-on-task" in his classroom and plots Tom's percent time-on-task for a baseline period of five days.

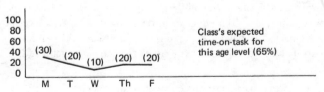

He calculates the mean and standard deviation for these days.

$$\text{Mean} = 20 \quad \text{S.D.} = \sqrt{\frac{200}{4}} = 7 \text{ (approximately)}$$

$$2\,(\text{S.D.}) = 14$$

2. He draws a two-standard deviation band above and below the mean and keeps observing and plotting points.

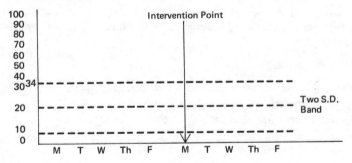

3. He intervenes by holding a series of parent conferences with the child present to discuss his concentration in school. He also asks Tom's teacher to award a gold star whenever Tom spends at least ten minutes on task.

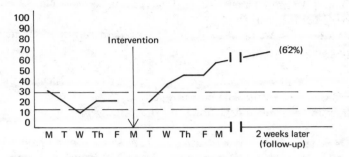

Tom's time-on-task has improved markedly. By Thursday there were two successive points outside the two-standard deviation band. A follow-up shows that Tom has remained close to the expected fourth-grader time-on-task performance.

The two-standard deviation band can also be used to set a target goal for an intervention. An intervention need not change a child's performance from 20 to 70 percent to be valuable. A significant shift can be obtained in the example above by any intervention that takes Tom beyond 34 percent time-on-task. We may hope to do better, but we certainly have not failed if we do at least 34 percent; unless, of course, the cost of the intervention is too great for the gains achieved.

WHAT IF OBSERVATIONS ARE NOT INDEPENDENT?

To discuss dependence, we will need to introduce a concept called "autocorrelation." You may be familiar with the concept of correlation. Two things are correlated if one is predictable from the other, or if knowledge about one thing reduces your uncertainty about the other. With data over time we use the concept of autocorrelation. If data over time are autocorrelated, then we can predict what will be happening at some time in the future just by knowing the past. At least by knowing the past we can reduce our uncertainty about the future, if the data are autocorrelated. First we need to find out if the data are autocorrelated and then we need to *transform* the data until the transformed data are not autocorrelated.

Calculating Autocorrelation

For a time series we can graph a scatterplot of the data. Suppose we are observing the frequency of a nervous tic. Figure 16.5 is a plot of that frequency for seventy hours of observation while the subject was awake.

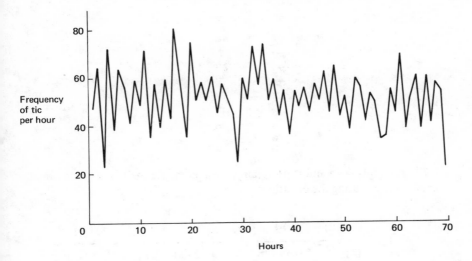

Figure 16.5. Frequency of a tic plotted per hour.

We can create scatterplots of these data by plotting an observation at time t on one axis of the graph, and the consecutive observation at time $t + 1$ on the other axis.

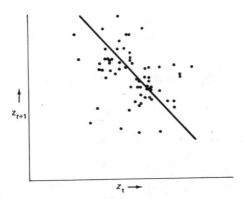

Fig 16.6. Scatterplot showing lag-1 autocorrelation.

We can see that these data show a *negative* autocorrelation. This means that a high frequency hour is likely to be followed by a lower frequency hour. Similarly, a lower frequency hour is likely to be followed by a higher frequency hour. In this scatterplot a correlation coefficient can be calculated. This coefficient is called the *first-order autocorrelation* coefficient because observations one time unit apart are paired for correlation. The table below illustrates this pairing:

t	$t+1$
observation #1	#2
#2	#3
#3	#4
#4	#5
#5	#6
#6	#7
•	•
•	•
•	•

Using this table and scattergram we can compute the first-order correlation coefficient r_1, using the equation:

$$r_1 = \frac{(z_1 - \bar{z})(z_2 - \bar{z}) + (z_2 - \bar{z})(z_3 - \bar{z}) + \ldots + (z_{N-1} - \bar{z})(z_N - \bar{z})}{(z_1 - \bar{z})^2 + (z_2 - \bar{z})^2 + \ldots + (z_N - \bar{z})^2}$$

Example: $z_1 = 2, z_2 = 2, z_3 = 3, z_4 = 5, N = 4$
$\bar{z} = (2 + 2 + 3 + 5)/4 = 3$

$z_1 - \bar{z} = -1$

$z_2 - \bar{z} = -1$

$z_3 - \bar{z} = 0$

$z_4 - \bar{z} = 2$

$r_1 = \dfrac{(-1)(-1) + (-1)(0) + (0)(2)}{1 + 1 + 0 + 4}$

$r_1 = \dfrac{1}{6} = .17$

The Correlogram

Similarly we can pair observations two time units apart:

t	$t+2$
observation#1	#3
#2	#4
#3	#5
#4	#6
•	•
•	•
•	•

The correlation coefficient we calculate would be called r_2, *the autocorrelation coefficient of lag-2.* For the tic frequency data, the lag-2 scatterplot would show a positive autocorrelation.

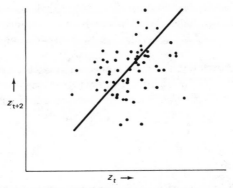

Figure 16.7. Scatterplot showing lag-2 autocorrelation.

We can continue calculating r_3, r_4, and so on. The correlogram is a plot of these correlation coefficients as a function of the lag. The general equation for the correlation coefficient of lag k is:

$$r_k = \left.\sum_{t=1}^{N-k} (z_t - \bar{z})(z_{t+k} - \bar{z}) \middle/ \sum_{t=1}^{N} (z_t - \bar{z})^2\right.$$

For the frequency of tics data the correlogram is given below.

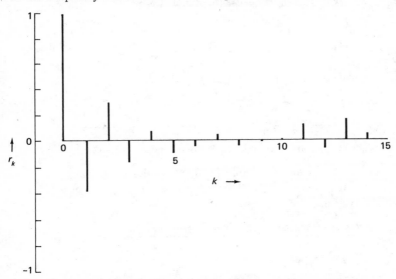

Figure 16.8. Correlogram showing the autocorrelation coefficient plotted as a function of lag.

An approximate test given by Bartlett (1946) to test whether r_k is significantly different from zero (at the .05 level), assuming observations are independent, is that r_k is effectively zero if it is less than $2/\sqrt{N}$, where N is the number of observations.

For most of the data we have seen in behavioral research it is only necessary to compute the first-order autocorrelation coefficient and see if it is significantly nonzero. If this finding is generally true, then the procedures above are greatly simplified.

Using Autocorrelation

If r_k is not significantly different from zero, then the observations are statistically independent and we can use the Shewart procedure. What does one do if r_k is greater than $2/\sqrt{N}$? The answer is that the data have to be transformed. Our goal is for the transformed data to have nonsignificant r_k.

Common Transformations

Eliminating trend   One way observations can be dependent is if there is a trend in the data. In this case the data do not oscillate around a constant value. The data may be transformed to eliminate a linear trend by using a transformation called the *first differences transformation.* Consider the data below:

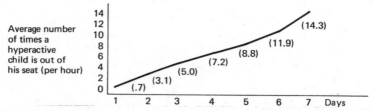

Figure 16.10.   Daily average out-of-seat frequencies for a hyperactive child.

These data show an increasing trend and r_k will be significantly nonzero. A first-differences transformation would create a new set of data by subtracting consecutive observations.

Transformed data	Transformation
2.4	3.1 − .7
1.9	5.0 − 3.1
2.2	7.2 − 5.0
1.6	8.8 − 7.2
3.1	11.9 − 8.8
2.4	14.3 − 11.9

These data are plotted below and represent increases or decreases in out-of-seat frequency from hour to hour. Note that this graph oscillates around a constant mean of approximately 2.27. The transformation may have to be applied again if there is still a trend in the transformed data.

Each time the transformation is performed we can calculate r_k and use Bartlett's test.

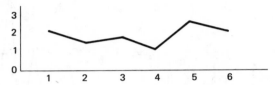

Figure 16.11. Elimination of trend with a first-differences transformation.

Another useful transformation is called the *moving average transformation.* In this transformation successive observations are averaged. We can average observations in groups of two, three, or more. For example, instead of plotting daily frequencies of a behavior, we can plot weekly averages. We can take any weighted sum of any group of observations and arrive at a moving average transformation. This transformation works to *smooth* data that are wildly oscillating. It may also reduce the autocorrelation coefficients.

Smoothing   A moving average process smooths a time series by plotting the average of a set of points. For example, we can plot the average of every two consecutive points below:

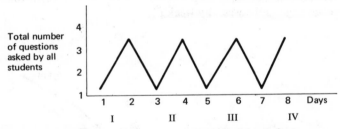

Figure 16.12. Hypothetical frequency of questions asked by students.

(Plot the average of days 1 and 2, then the average of days 3, 4, and so on.)

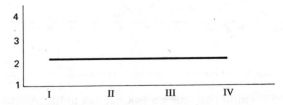

Figure 16.13. Smoothing using a moving average transformation.

In the following graph, the teacher plotted her class's average percent time attending to a task (time-on-task). After the first four weeks she began rewarding students for completing their tasks. She plotted the points each day and then used a moving average process to compare weeks 1–4 with weeks 5–7.

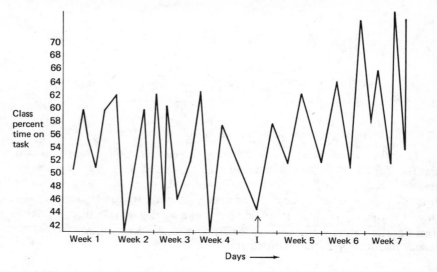

Figure 16.14.   Average percent time-on-task for a classroom plotted over time.

The average for week one was $\dfrac{50 + 58 + 54 + 50 + 58}{5} = 54$ percent time on task. The graph below gives the week by week plot:

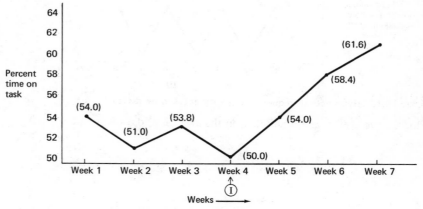

Figure 16.15.   Smoothing using a moving average transformation.

The effects of the intervention become a bit clearer due to the smoothing process.

SUMMARY

Our objective was to transform the data so that r_k is nonsignificant using the Bartlett test. Note that we were doing this so that we could use Shewart's method for the *transformed data*. Because of this we caution the reader to apply the same transformation to the data after the baseline and to the data after the intervention. *All the data must be transformed in the same way.*

The flow chart below summarizes this section:

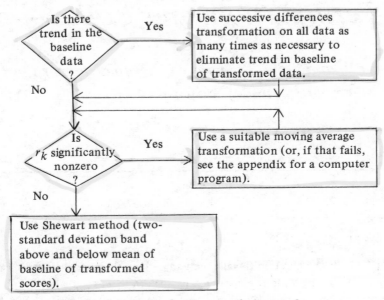

Figure 16.16. This flow chart summarizes how to assess the impact of an intervention graphically.

XVII

Planning Transfer of Training, Termination, and Follow-up

K4. and K5. Transfer of therapeutic learning; termination and follow-up.

TRANSFER

PSYCHOTHERAPY has traditionally ignored perhaps the most important aspect of treatment: transfer of learning from therapy to extratherapy situations. Rather than programming for generalization, transfer has been left to chance. Goldstein, Heller, and Sechrest (1966) presented an excellent discussion and theoretical rationale of this issue. We refer the reader to their book for more detail than we can present here. However, we will discuss three general ways that transfer of learning may be enhanced.

Learning a General Principle

It is helpful to learn a general principle that can be applied to extratherapy situations. In educational research, teaching a general principle before requiring the demonstration of a specific skill enhances performance in that skill (Judd, 1902; Hendrickson and Schroeder, 1941; Woodrow, 1927; and Ulmer, 1939).

Example: For impulsive children, self-control can be enchanced by teaching the child to instruct himself to stop and think before responding (Leiblum, 1971; Palkes, Stewart and Kahana, 1968).

For married couples, the general principle of paraphrasing and checking out the accuracy of what the listener understands can be used to improve communication in real-life situations.

In organizations where work teams are experiencing decreased productivity, the general principle of concensus in decision making can be used to improve morale and productivity.

Sampling from the Population

Transfer from therapy to extratherapy situations will be increased by sampling from the population of situations to which we want the response to generalize. To maximize transfer, there should be some degree of overlearning.

In assertiveness training, a domain of situations the subject is likely to encounter is created. Role-playing techniques are used to develop and strengthen assertive responses in situations which can be sampled at random from the domain. A patient may have difficulty being assertive with his spouse. However, in order to strengthen the likelihood of assertive responses in other situations as well, it is useful to have him practice being assertive with salespeople, employees, and relatives.

One of the gains from this type of procedure has been suggested by the learning set experiments of Harlow (1949). In the first situation presented to the patient, he is learning a specific behavior to a specific stimulus. In later situations, the subject may be learning a strategy that can be applied to novel situations.

One of the implications of this method is that transfer from therapy to extratherapy situations will be greater if: (1) therapy is conducted with the system (physical and human) in which the problem occurs, and (2) therapy introduces a variety of "simulations" of real-life situations in which the patient will ultimately have to respond.

Boocock and Schild (1968) reviewed educational research on the effects of using simulation games and simulated environments on learning, attitude toward learning, and transfer to novel situations. They presented an example of the use of simulation in learning which may be of interest. In learning the principles of economics by games and simulation, the student was given a problem in which he pretended that he was the pharaoh's economic advisor. As advisor he was given some basic data on the kingdom and asked to make some economic decisions. After his decision, he was given next year's basic data. The wrong decision (for example, storing too much grain) may have resulted in decimating the population. This way the student inductively learns the principles of sound economic decision making. Simulation methods were found superior to traditional teaching approaches in attitude change, retention, and transfer (Boocock and Schild, 1968, p. 142).

The objective of simulations is to teach the subject strategy which will enable him to generate behaviors appropriate to situations he encounters while learning. Transfer rests on the hypothesis that having learned the strategy will enable the subject to generate an appropriate behavior in novel situations. Assertiveness, for example, may be viewed as a strategy which allows the subject to generate behaviors that get him what he wants. With a pushy salesman, this may amount to saying "no" firmly. However, other situational contexts may involve different behaviors that also result in getting the subject his rights.

Examples

1. Learning of interpersonal skills may be strengthened and there will be greater transfer if therapy is provided by more than one therapist (for example, the use of co-therapists, multi-impact therapy) and if group therapy is employed as a treatment modality.

2. Therapy within the system in which the problem occurs can be illustrated by the increased interest in family therapy, school consultation, and community psychology. Redl and Wineman (1957) discussed the use of a program of crisis-intervention for behavior problems occurring in the classroom. In this procedure, the therapist teaches the child to monitor his behavior, understand his autonomy as a decision maker, and appreciate the consequences of his decisions. These learnings occur in a wide variety of situations which are generated by the real-life system.

Goldstein, Heller, and Sechrest (1966, p. 230) said, "It is interesting how selective psychiatry and psychology have been in their borrowings from the medical model; the standard professional office is much admired but house calls are not."

3. Therapy can be made to simulate real-life situations. This is currently being done in a number of ways. For example, in the aversive treatment of alcoholism, a portable bar is often part of the therapeutic environment (Schaefer, Sobell, and Mills, 1971). Halfway houses and day-care facilities for adult psychiatric patients have been used to advantage and simulations in which anxiety producing situations are anticipated can be used to decrease the threat-value of these situations.

Learning to Discriminate Differences and Recognize Commonalities

Transfer of therapeutic learning will be maximized if the client learns to discriminate the differences and recognize the commonalities among situations and responses. Mediated generalization refers to "making diverse stimuli equivalent by attaching the same cue-producing response or label to them. For example, if a therapy patient can learn to recognize and label his feelings in certain situations as 'hostile,' then in any other situation in which the same label is employed the same responses should occur." (Goldstein, Heller, and Sechrest, 1966, p. 217)

Mediated discrimination refers to the use of labels to enhance the distinctiveness of stimuli (for example, "when a patient learns to label certain of his fears as 'unjustified' so that he distinguishes them from realistic fears," p. 219).

For example, a good deal of psychotherapy places strong emphasis on expressing and analyzing negative responses such as hostility, self-derogation, and incompetence. The expression of unexpressed feelings may be essential. However, there is some evidence that focusing on negative responses will increase their occurrence. In an experiment by McFall (1970), subjects monitored instances of smoking a cigarette or refraining from smoking. Subjects who monitored smoking increased the frequency of their smoking. Gottman and McFall (1972) replicated these findings for the response of classroom participation in a class of potential high school dropouts. Todd and Kelley (1972) reported an increase in self-esteem following the extensive use of the symbolic reinforcement of covert positive self-statements.

The therapist has a choice of tactics for dealing with a client's problem. For example, a client with a "mental block" to remembering important events may be helped to investigate the reasons for the block, its etiology, and past history; or the therapist can teach the client how to remember, using mnemonics, for instance. Getting a client to express his hostility is seen by many therapists as having an important cathartic effect. There is some evidence, however, that this process disinhibits aggressive behavior in other, unacceptable situations. A behavioral approach would attempt to teach a client to discriminate the occasions and situations acceptable for aggressive display. There is also some evidence that therapies which emphasize the exploration of negative responses reinforce the client's playing the "sick role." A final example of this point is the contention by analytically oriented therapists that a child who has suffered the loss of a parent needs to grieve and mourn the loss before he will be able psychologically to relinquish the dead person and invest energies in other relationships. An alternative approach to this problem is to help the child find satisfaction and gratification from people in his present environment.

TERMINATION AND FOLLOW-UP

The issue of termination has been discussed as an intuitive question (Wolberg, 1954) which depends on a large variety of factors. Termination is greatly simplified if psychotherapy has been designed to monitor the progress toward unambiguous goals. Several questions are usually discussed in connection with termination:

1. *When should you terminate?* Psychoanalytically oriented therapists might argue that psychotherapy is a never-ending process since personal growth is lifelong. Goallessness has even been cited as the procedural stance of technical analytic work (Wallerstein, 1965). However, if therapy continues too long, the threat of excessive dependency becomes a major issue. If therapy ends too abruptly, before learning has transferred to extratherapy situations, therapy may be of little enduring value to the client. The assessment of how long is made more precise by the evaluation of change toward observable specifically stated therapy goals.

2. What criteria should be used to terminate?

3. Who determines when therapy should end?

4. How should therapy end? (gradually, abruptly?)

There is no ideal way to terminate, or even a "right" or "wrong" way to handle this difficult decision. Termination is an individual matter and depends on the contract established between client and therapist in the early weeks of therapy.

When therapy is to end depends on the goals established at the initiation of treatment. Possibly there may be more work to be accomplished between client and therapist. However, therapy is not designed to handle all of the problems. present and potential, that the client faces. Resolution of the original difficulties to the mutual satisfaction of client and therapist is a good criterion for the termination of treatment. Ideally, the client, at the termination of treatment, not only has resolved some specific difficulties but has learned methods for tackling problems in the future (see Section K4, planning for transfer and generalization).

The decision to terminate should be made jointly by client and therapist. There are times when the client, perhaps because of realistic financial pressures or time pressures, might want to terminate before the therapist feels he is ready. Alternatively, it is possible that the client might be reluctant to terminate, even after his initial complaints have been resolved. He may be reluctant to relinquish the supportive, protective, and reinforcing attention he derives from the therapy hour. Or he may feel threatened by his ability to handle problems independently and successfully in the future. The idea of termination may bring up disturbing memories and feelings associated with separations from important figures in his past.

The therapist might also have difficulties terminating with a patient because of his own desire to protect, nurture, and be significant in the life of another person, because of the reinforcement he derives from the client's respect for him, and because of his own difficulties in separating from someone he has experienced a close, meaningful relationship with. Certain reactions and feelings are a natural accompaniment of the decision to end treatment. Both therapist and patient might feel sad that their relationship is ending. The client might be expected to feel somewhat anxious about his ability to handle his problems alone in the future. He may also be somewhat relieved that he has successfully resolved a difficulty and can operate independently now. In the last weeks of therapy, it is useful to discuss these feelings. In leaving, the therapist and client can separate real issues from fantasized and unrealistic issues. Reviewing what has been accomplished over the course of therapy, identifying the skills the client has to deal with future difficulties, and anticipating problems that might arise after treatment will facilitate termination and reduce anxiety. The client might be warned that some "relapse" may occur which will give him a chance to exercise his new learning. He may also be assured that learning continues after termination. He will develop and extend the skills he has learned and experience success with difficult situations.

Following discussion of termination, it is useful to set a termination date some weeks in the future and then end treatment with the understanding that should serious problems arise in the future, the client is free to call the therapist for consultation. Setting a definite date reduces the ambiguity surrounding the termination. It also provides some pressure to accomplish the goals established and allows time for discussion of the feelings of both client and therapist regarding termination.

Finally, at termination, the therapist should arrange for a follow-up interview either three, six, or twelve months in the future to assess how the client is performing. Lederer and Jackson (1968) have married couples return for periodic "checkups" every few months for a year or so after termination. It may be useful for the therapist to think seriously about termination several sessions in advance and to think of it in terms of leaving the client with a "Christmas gift" of behaviors he can apply to problematic situations that may arise in the future. Then, several sessions before termination the therapist and client can discuss a "phasing out" process in which the client has greater and greater responsibility for proofreading his own behavior and problem solving. The therapist should program his own behavior to minimize his own interventions. More and more therapy can be assigned as homework while phasing out. Checkups can be planned to assess the success of the decision to terminate. A good indication of a successful termination occurs when an ex-client finds that he has far more important things to do than come to therapy and when therapy checkup sessions are just a big pain in the neck to the client.

APPENDIX

A Computer Program

For the analysis of the interrupted time-series experiment based on the IMA (1, 1) model[1]

INTRODUCTION

THIS APPENDIX ASSUMES you know what a *t*-test is and how to use it. If that is not the case, see Gottman and Clasen (1972). It is designed as a manual with two objectives in mind. The first objective is to teach the reader how to make use of a computer program for the analysis of the interrupted time-series experiment. A computer program developed by Glass and Maguire (1968) and based on Box and Tiao (1965) will be listed at the end of this appendix. The reader will learn how to set up data for using the program and how to interpret some of the output. The second objective of this appendix is to give the reader an understanding of how the computer program works.

An interrupted time-series experiment consists of a series of observations (denoted by O's) preceding and following an intervention (denoted by an I). The observations can be a mean averaged over subjects, observation on a single subject over time (unit repetitive), or observations of an intact organizational unit observed over time (for example, a second-grade classroom) with different subjects (unit replicative).

The reader is urged to consult other sources for a full discussion of time-series methods. For detailed discussion of different time-series designs, sources of invalidity, and a general introduction to time series see Glass, Willson, and Gottman (1973). This source also presents a computer program developed by Victor Willson

---

[1] Developed by John Mordechai Gottman, Indiana University.

based on another time-series model, the IMA (2, 2) model. For a general introduction to the mathematics of time-series analysis (but not the interrupted time-series experiment), the reader is referred to Box and Jenkins (1970). For a general method of analyzing the interrupted time-series experiment for a wide class of time-series models see Kepka (1972). For a discussion of N-of-one designs applied to psychotherapy research see Gottman (1973).

OUTPUT

The salient output of the IMA (1, 1) program listed in this appendix are three graphs. Two of these are Student t values graphed as a function of a model parameter called *gamma*. The third is a graph of the likelihood function, which is also a function of gamma. This manual will teach you how to read the table that presents these graphs.

Change in Slope and Level

Following an intervention there may be an immediate drop in the level of the series. There may also be a change in the drift or slope of the series. Figure A.1 presents the four possibilities for change in these parameters.

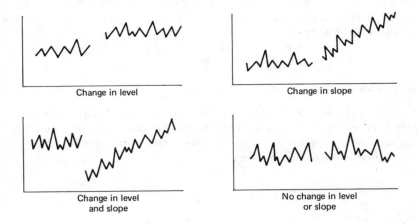

Figure A.1.   Level and slope in the interrupted time-series experiment.

Likelihood Function

Just as in regression we try to find the parameter values that *minimize* a sum of squares of deviations, we can equivalently find those parameter values that maximize a function called *the likelihood function.* See Figure A.2.

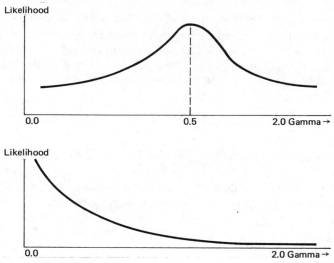

Figure A.2.   Likelihood function.

In the top graph in Figure A.2 the value of gamma which maximizes the likelihood function is gamma = 0.5. In the bottom graph the value of gamma which maximizes the likelihood function is gamma = 0.0. This value of gamma is called the *maximum likelihood gamma.*

Student's t's for Change in Level and Slope

Once the maximum likelihood gamma is found, the appropriate *t* values for change in level and slope are read from the table and looked up as any *t* would be using degrees of freedom, df=N-3, where N is the total number of observations (preintervention plus postintervention).

Output Table

The table of interest has eleven columns and 199 rows. Each row represents the model parameter, gamma, incremented by 0.01 with a range $0 \leq gamma \leq 2$. See Figure A.3 for an abbreviated table. The first column gives values of gamma. The next column of interest is Column 6 labeled "T for change." It represents student's t values for change in level. The next column of interest is Column 10, also labeled "T for Change." It represents student's *t* values for change in slope. The eleventh column is labeled "Scaled Posterior" and represents values of the maximum likelihood function.

Gamma	Residual Variance	Level	T for Level	Change in Level	T for Change	Slope	T for Slope	Change in Slope	T for Change	Scaled Posterior	(Maximum Likelihood)
.01	.568	-24.30	-6.55	-52.83	-7.22	35.03	10.26	52.87	7.39	22.16	←Maximum
.02	.574	- 6.78	-3.37	-26.39	-7.00	17.52	10.22	26.43	7.37	5.57	
.03	.579	- 9.54	- .65	-17.57	-6.76	11.69	10.14	17.61	7.34	2.50	
—	—	—	—	—	—	—	—	—	—	—	
—	—	—	—	—	—	—	—	—	—	—	
1.99	.698	7.33	34.27	- 1.19	-3.82	.28	1.42	.11	.34	.00	

Fig A.3. Partial output table (taken from Glass and Maguire's, 1968, analysis of German divorce law data, df = N-3.)

Reading the Table

To read the table follow these steps:

1. Find the row (or the rows) for which the "scaled posterior" is a maximum.
2. Read Column 6 and Column 10 for that row (or those rows).

For the data of Figure A.3 maximum likelihood gamma is in the first row (scaled posterior is greatest at gamma = 0.01). So T for Change in level (Column 6)= -7.22 and T for Change in slope (Column 10) = 7.39.

Example

An experiment by Gottman and Asher intervened on the playground to modify peer social interaction in the classroom. This experiment will be described here because their data illustrate the interpretation of time-series data.

Method

Subjects: In a third-grade classroom, five subjects were identified by the teacher as problem children and five subjects were selected at random from a class of twenty-seven students.

Variables: An observer recorded the frequency of the following behaviors: (a) alone and working; (b) alone and not working (daydreaming, withdrawn); (c) positive verbal interaction with peers; (d) hitting, pushing, sparring with peers; (e) negative verbal interaction with peers; and (f) interaction with teacher. The observer checked the appropriate behavior every three seconds, scanning down a randomized list of names of the ten subjects. An acceptable interobserver agreement of 82.5 percent was achieved using this taxonomy of interactive behavior.

Procedure: The teacher's objective was to increase positive verbal interaction and to decrease hitting and negative verbal interaction in the classroom. The children played a game on the playground they called "smear." In this game one student got the ball; it was his job to hold on to the ball and everyone else's job to get the ball away, at any cost. It was felt that this game might be modified to increase cooperative play. It was hoped that learnings would generalize to the classroom. Students suggested a voluntary game that involved passing a ball as often as possible, a game analogous to an old game called "hot potato." Noncooperative players were not permitted to play. At first the teacher coached the children and then the children began coaching each other. The game became popular and it was the teacher's impression that there was considerable carryover of good feelings to the classroom.

Results

The analysis of the results of this intervention have been presented in some detail by Gottman and Asher (1972). For the purpose of illustration we will discuss only the results for the variable alone and working ("alone positive"). This variable is a good indicator of the effects of the intervention on increasing interaction time. As time spent alone decreases, time spent interacting with peers increased. Figure A.4 shows a sharp drop in time spent alone (t level = -5.14, p < 0.01). The figure also indicates a return to base *indicating that the effect was only temporarily effective.* This return to base is indicated by a significant increase in slope after the initial drop in level (t slope = 4.46, p. < 0.01).

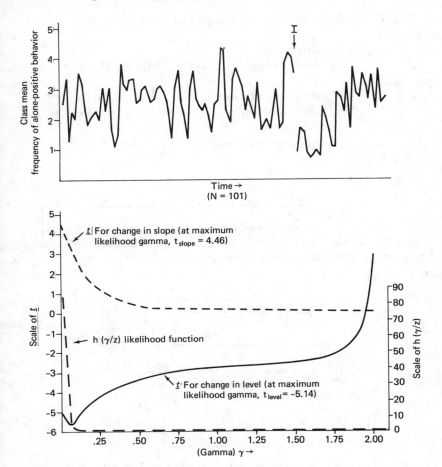

Figure A.4.   Interrupted time-series experiment.

Figure A.4 presents the data (top graph), the likelihood function (long dotted line, bottom graph), Student's t values for a change in level (sold line, bottom graph), and Student's t values for a change in slope (small dotted line, bottom graph). These graphs were constructed using Column 11, Column 6, and Column 10 respectively.

INPUT

To prepare the data and control cards, see the comment cards of the program listing. Suppose the data were 5.6, 5.7, 5.4, for preintervention, and 6.3, 6.2, and 6.0 for postintervention.

Card 1:   Col. 1-2: put 01 since only one problem is to be run. Other columns: blank

Card 2:   Col. 2-80: title of problem

Card 3:   Col. 1-80: format of data cards in form (FORMAT); for this example it is (6 F2.1)

Card 4:   Col. 1-4: number of pretreatment observations; in this case 0003
            Col. 5-8: number of posttreatment observations; in this case 0003
            Col. 9: punch a zero

Card 5:   Data card without separation of pre and post data. Punch the numbers as follows:

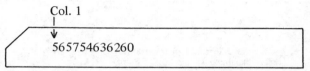

Col. 1

565754636260

Card 6, etc.:   Following the cards above are the cards of the computer program.

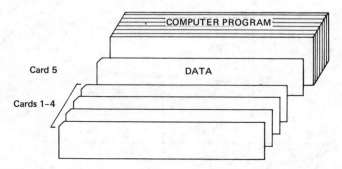

COMPUTER PROGRAM

Card 5   DATA

Cards 1-4

In front of and behind this arrangement, you will have to put the appropriate "systems cards" which your computing facility requires for using an intact program. You can get help on setting up these cards from your computing center.

How the Computer Program Works

The basic equations for this program are given and discussed in Glass, Willson, and Gottman (1973). The basic problem in analyzing data over time is that these data are usually *dependent.* This means that to some extent it is possible to predict an observation from the past values of the time series. Dependency even to a moderate degree has serious consequences for how confident you can be that an intervention really had an effect greater than chance variation in the data. It is no simple problem to deal with this dependency.

It is simple to measure the dependency by using the concept of auto-correlation (the correlation of past with future values lagged a specified number of time units). Using autocorrelation it is possible to specify *models* for time-series data. A model is a mathematical representation which tries to approximate the obtained data. The computer program of this appendix uses a particular model. Any model is really a set of assumptions about the data.

With a model a set of transformations can be specified which permits one to decompose the observed time series $Z(t)$ into the sum of two parts, a *deterministic* component, $X(t)$, and an independent random component, $a(t)$. This is expressed in an equation

$$Z(t) = X(t) + a(t)$$

The t here represents time. The computer program of this appendix assumes that $X(t)$ is a straight line with a level and slope (which can change as a result of the intervention).

Expressed in this transformed form, the equation can be "solved" using an equation called "the general linear model." Kepka (1972) derived a general way of obtaining these transformations for a broad class of time-series models suggested by Box and Jenkins (1970).

Basically then what the program does is to assume a model [the IMA $(1, 1)$ model] which provides a transformation of the data to the form of the equation above, and then solves the equation using the "general linear model" solution.

LISTING OF THE PROGRAM

```
        PROGRAMTIMESER(INPUT,OUTPUT,TAPE5=INPUT,TAPE6=OUTPUT)
*DECK TSX-3
C TIME SERIES INCORPORATING CHANGE IN DRIFT
C PARAMETER CARD ONE  COLS. 1,2  NR=NUMBER OF PROBLEMS TO BE RUN
C CARDS 2,3,4 ARE REQUIRED FOR EACH PROBLEM TO BE RUN
C CARD 2 COLS.2-80   TITLE OF PROBLEM
C CARD 3 COLS 1-80 FORMAT FOR DATA CARDS..IN THE FORM (FORMAT)
C CARD 4 COLS. 1-4 NUMBER OF PRE TREATMENT MEASURES. COLS. 5-8 NUMBER OF
C POST TREATMENT MEASURES.  COL. 9. 1 IF CORRELOGRAM REQUIRED, 0 OTHERWISE
C CARD 5 ETC. DATA CARDS FOR FIRST PROBLEM NO SEPERATION BETWEEN PRE AND POST
C TREATMENT DATA
        DIMENSION Z(500),Y(500),X(500,4),XTXIN(4,4),XTX(4,4),XTY(4)
        DIMENSION THETA(4),FMT(18),TITLE(18),PD(200),XOUT(201,11)
        DIMENSION SF(4),T(4),B(4,1)
        DIMENSION XX(200,10),DELCON(200,5),FNAM(5,5),G1(5),G2(5),G3(5),G4(
       15),G5(5),G6(5),G7(5),G8(5),G9(5),G10(5)
        DATA G1/20HT..CHANGE IN LEVEL   /
        DATA G2/20HT..CHANGE IN SLOPE   /
        DATA G3/20HSCALED POSTERIOR     /
        DATA G4/20HLOWER 99 PERCENT     /
        DATA G5/20HLOWER 95 PERCENT     /
        DATA G6/20HDELTA                /
        DATA G7/20HUPPER 95 PERCENT     /
        DATA G8/20HUPPER 99 PERCENT     /
        XXCK=1.0E-15
        NRR=0
        READ(5,36)NR
   36   FORMAT(I2)
   39   READ(5,1)(TITLE(I),I=1,18)
    1   FORMAT(18A4)
        JK=0
        NIT=0
        G=0.01
        NRR=NRR+1
        WRITE(6,37)NRR
   37   FORMAT(//9H PROBLEM I2//)
        WRITE(6,1)(TITLE(I),I=1,18)
        READ(5,1)(FMT(I),I=1,18)
        READ(5,3)N1,N2,NCC
    3   FORMAT(2I4,I1)
        NTOT=N1+N2
        READ(5,FMT)(Z(I),I=1,NTOT)
        WRITE(6,601)N1,N2
  601   FORMAT(//8X,4H N1=I3,4H N2=I3//)
        WRITE(6,602)
  602   FORMAT(15H        INPUT DATA)
        WRITE(6,600)(Z(I),I=1,N1)
  600   FORMAT(5(1XF13.5))
        NNN=N1+1
        WRITE(6,603)(Z(I),I=NNN,NTOT)
  603   FORMAT(//5(1XF13.5))
        IF(NCC)702,701,702
  702   CALL CORREL (N1,N2,Z)
  701   CONTINUE
        WRITE(6,666)
  666   FORMAT(1H0)
        WRITE(6,22)
   22   FORMAT(1X114H        RESIDUAL                   T FOR        CHANGE IN  T
       1 FOR               T FOR        CHANGE IN    T FOR        SCALED)
        WRITE(6,2022)
 2022   FORMAT(1X117HGAMMA     VARIANCE       LEVEL        LEVEL        LEVEL
       1CHANGE     SLOPE       SLOPE        SLOPE       CHANGE      POSTERIOR)
   25   CONTINUE
C CALCULATION OF Y SCORES FROM THE DATA ..CHECK FOR  UNDERFLOW WHEN GAMMA
C IS 1.0 AND  Y(N) IS NEARLY EQUAL TO Y(N-1)
        Y(1)=Z(1)
        DO 5 I=2,NTOT
```

```
      II=I-1
      YY=ABS(Y(II))
      IF(YY-XXCK)42,42,45
  45  IF(YY-.000001)40,40,41
  40  GG=ABS(1.0-G)
      IF(GG-.001)42,42,41
  42  Y(I)=Z(I)-Z(II)
      GO TO 5
  41  Y(I)=(Z(I)-Z(II))+(1.0-G)*Y(II)
   5  CONTINUE
C CALCULATION OF WEIGHTS. IF ABSOLUTE VALUE OF X IS LESS THAN 1.0E-15, THEN IT
C IS SET EQUAL TO ZERO TO PREVENT UNDERFLOW
      DO 1000 I=1,NTOT
 1000 X(I,1)=1.0
      DO 2000 I=1,N1
 2000 X(I,2)=0.0
      NNN1=N1+1
      DO 2001 I=NNN1,NTOT
 2001 X(I,2)=1.0
      X(1,3)=1.0
      X(2,3)=1.0-G
      DO 6 I=3,NTOT
      II=I-1
      X(I,3)=X(2,3)*X(II,3)
      XXX=ABS(X(I,3))
      IF(XXCK-XXX)6,6,32
  32  X(I,3)=0.0
   6  CONTINUE
      DO 7 I=1,N1
   7  X(I,4)=0.0
      NN=N1+1
      DO 8 I=NN,NTOT
      II=I-N1
      X(I,4)=X(II,3)
      XXX=ABS(X(I,4))
      IF(XXCK-XXX)8,8,33
  33  X(I,4)=0.0
   8  CONTINUE
      DO 11 I=1,4
      DO 11 J=1,4
      XTX(I,J)=0.0
  11  XTXIN(I,J)=0.0
C CALCULATION OF X TRANSPOSE X INVERSE
      DO 4050 I=1,4
      DO 4050 J=1,4
      DO 4050 K=1,NTOT
 4050 XTX(I,J)=XTX(I,J)+X(K,I)*X(K,J)
      DO 2002 I=1,4
      DO 2002 J=1,4
 2002 XTXIN(I,J)=XTX(I,J)
      DO 4061 I=1,4
 4061 XTY(I)=0.0
      DO 4062 I=1,4
      DO 4062 J=1,NTOT
 4062 XTY(I)=XTY(I)+X(J,I)*Y(J)
      DO 2003 I=1,4
 2003 B(I,1)=XTY(I)
      CALL MATINV(XTXIN,4,B,1,DET)
      DO 2020 I=1,4
 2020 THETA(I)=B(I,1)
      DO 2004 I=1,4
 2004 SE(I)=XTXIN(I,I)
      FNTOT=NTOT
      YTY=0.0
C CALCULATION OF THE RESIDUAL VARIANCE
      DO 18 I=1,NTOT
  18  YTY=YTY+Y(I)**2
      DO 31 I=1,4
  31  XTY(I)=0.0
```

```
      DO 19 J=1,4
      DO 19 I=1,4
19    XTY(J)=XTY(J)+THETA(I)*XTX(I,J)
      FITVAR=0.0
      DO 20 I=1,4
20    FITVAR=FITVAR+XTY(I)*THETA(I)
      S=YTY-FITVAR
      S=S/(FNTOT-4.0)
C CALCULATION OF THE STANDARD ERRORS OF DELTA AND MU
      DO 2010 I=1,4
      SE(I)=SQRT(S*SE(I))
2010  T(I)=THETA(I)/SE(I)
C CALCULATION OF THE POSTERIOR DISTRIBUTION... LOGS ARE USED TO PREVENT
C OVERFLOW
      SK=ALOG(S)
      DET=ALOG(DET)
      H=(-.5*DET)-(.5*(FNTOT-4.0)*SK)
      H=.4342945*H
      JK=JK+1
      XOUT(JK,1)=G
      XOUT(JK,2)=S
      XOUT(JK,3)=THETA(3)
      XOUT(JK,4)=T(3)
      XOUT(JK,5)=THETA(4)
      XOUT(JK,6)=T(4)
      XOUT(JK,7)=THETA(1)
      XOUT(JK,8)=T(1)
      XOUT(JK,9)=THETA(2)
      XOUT(JK,10)=T(2)
      IF(NTOT-30)1004,1005,1005
1005  DELCON(JK,1)=THETA(4)-2.58*SE(4)
      DELCON(JK,2)=THETA(4)-1.96*SE(4)
      DELCON(JK,3)=THETA(4)
      DELCON(JK,4)=THETA(4)+1.96*SE(4)
      DELCON(JK,5)=THETA(4)+2.58*SE(4)
1004  NIT=NIT+1
      PD(NIT)=H
C INCREMENT GAMMA BY .01 AND ITERATE
      G=G+1.00000000E-02
      IF(NIT-199)30,30,26
30    GO TO 25
26    CONTINUE
C FIND MAXIMUM VALUE OF THE POSTERIOR
      FIN=PD(1)
      DO 506 I=2,199
      IF(FIN-PD(I))505,506,506
505   FIN=PD(I)
506   CONTINUE
C RESCALE POSTERIOR BY DIVIDING ALL VALUES OF THE POSTERIOR BY THE MAX VALUE
      DO 507 I=1,199
      PD(I)=PD(I)-FIN
      YY=ABS(PD(I))
      IF(YY-35.0)509,508,508
508   PD(I)=0.0
      GO TO 507
509   PD(I)=PD(I)/.4342945
      PD(I)=EXP(PD(I))
507   CONTINUE
C CONVERT AREA OF THE POSTERIOR DISTRIBUTION TO UNIT AREA BY METHOD OF TRAPEZO
      AREA=0.0
      DO 511 I=2,199
      II=I-1
511   AREA=AREA+.005*(PD(I)+PD(II))
      DO 512 I=1,199
512   PD(I)=PD(I)/AREA
      DO 513 I=1,199
513   XOUT(I,11)=PD(I)
      DO 514 I=1,199
514   WRITE(6,23)(XOUT(I,J),J=1,11)
```

```
  23   FORMAT(1X,1F5.2,10(1XE10.3))
       DO 700 I=1,199
       XX(I,1)=XOUT(I,5)
       XX(I,2)=XOUT(I,9)
 700   XX(I,3)=XOUT(I,11)
       M=199
       N=3
       ISCALE=1
C TITLE FOR  PLOT OF THE POSTERIOR DISTRIBUTION AND FOR STUDENT T
       DO 760 I=1,5
       FNAM(1,I)=G1(I)
       FNAM(2,I)=G2(I)
 760   FNAM(3,I)=G3(I)
       CALL PLOT(M,N,ISCALE,XX,FNAM)
       N=5
C PLOT CONFIDENCE INTERVALS AROUND DELTA
       IF(NTOT-30)1007,1006,1006
1006 DO 1008 I=1,199
       DO 1008 J=1,5
1008 XX(I,J)=DELCON(I,J)
       DO 756 I=1,5
       FNAM(1,I)=G4(I)
       FNAM(2,I)=G5(I)
       FNAM(3,I)=G6(I)
       FNAM(4,I)=G7(I)
 756   FNAM(5,I)=G8(I)
       WRITE(6,1016)
1016 FORMAT(//34H CONFIDENCE INTERVALS AROUND DELTA)
       WRITE(6,1017)
1017 FORMAT(/3X,5HGAMMA,2X,52H LOWER 99   LOWER 95     DELTA      UPPER 95
     1    UPPER 99)
       DO 1019 I=1,199
1019 WRITE(6,1018)XOUT(I,1),(DELCON(I,J),J=1,5)
1018 FORMAT(3X,1F5.2,1X5E10.3)
       WRITE(6,1015)
1015 FORMAT(//1X,47H GRAPH OF CONFIDENCE INTERVALS AROUND DELTA HAT)
       CALL PLOT(M,N,ISCALE,XX,FNAM)
1007 NR=NR-1
       IF(NR)38,38,39
  38   CONTINUE
       STOP
       END




       SUBROUTINE CORREL (N1,N2,Z)
       DIMENSION Z(500),RLAG(400),Y(500),XX(200,10),FNAM(5,5)
       DIMENSION G9(5),G10(5)
       DATA G9/20HPRE TREATMENT DATA   /
       DATA G10/20HPOST TREATMENT DATA /
       NTOT=N1+N2
C PREPARATION OF TITLE FOR CORRELOGRAM PLOT
       DO 804 JJJ=1,4
       IND=JJJ
       IF(IND-2)805,806,807
 807   IF(IND-4)805,806,806
 805   CONTINUE
       DO 757 I=1,5
 757   FNAM(1,I)=G9(I)
       GO TO 808
 806   CONTINUE
       DO 758 I=1,5
 758   FNAM(1,I)=G10(I)
 808   CONTINUE
       GO TO (809,810,811,812),IND
C PREPARATION OF DATA TO CALCULATE AUTOCORRELATIONS FOR PRE TREATMENT DATA
 809 NLAG=N1
```

```
      NLOW=1
      NTOP=N1
      WRITE(6,813)
  813 FORMAT(//38H CORRELOGRAM OF PRE TREATMENT RAW DATA)
      GO TO 814
C PREPARATION OF DATA TO CALCULATE AUTOCORRELATIONS FOR POST TREATMENT DATA
  810 NLAG=N2
      NLOW=N1+1
      NTOP=NTOT
      WRITE(6,815)
  815 FORMAT(//39H CORRELOGRAM OF POST TREATMENT RAW DATA)
  814 II=0
      DO 706 I=NLOW,NTOP
      II=II+1
  706 Y(II)=Z(I)
      GO TO 709
C PREPARATION OF DATA TO CALCULATE AUTOCORRELATIONS FOR PRE TREATMENT
C DIFFERENCES  BETWEEN SUCCESSIVE OBSERVATIONS
  811 NLAG=N1-1
      NLOW=1
      NTOP=N1-1
      WRITE(6,800)
  800 FORMAT(//41H CORRELOGRAM OF PRE TREATMENT DIFFERENCES)
      GO TO 816
C PREPARATION OF DATA TO CALCULATE AUTOCORRELATIONS FOR POST TREATMENT
C DIFFERENCES  BETWEEN SUCCESSIVE OBSERVATIONS
  812 NLAG=N2-1
      NLOW=N1+1
      NTOP=NTOT-1
      WRITE(6,803)
  803 FORMAT(//42H CORRELOGRAM OF POST TREATMENT DIFFERENCES)
  816 II=0
      DO 707 I=NLOW,NTOP
      II=II+1
      IK=I+1
  707 Y(II)=Z(IK)-Z(I)
  709 JJ=NLAG*3/4
      DO 716 K=1,JJ
      NUP=NLAG-K
      CROS=0.0
      SUM1=0.0
      SUM2=0.0
      SUMS1=0.0
      SUMS2=0.0
      DO 703 I=1,NUP
      NIND=I+K
      CROS=CROS+Y(I)*Y(NIND)
      SUM1=SUM1+Y(I)
      SUM2=SUM2+Y(NIND)
      SUMS1=SUMS1+Y(I)*Y(I)
  703 SUMS2=SUMS2+Y(NIND)*Y(NIND)
      FNUP=NUP
      DNUM=CROS-(SUM1*SUM2)/FNUP
      DEN=(SUMS1-(SUM1*SUM1)/FNUP)*(SUMS2-(SUM2*SUM2)/FNUP)
      DEN=SQRT(DEN)
      RLAG(K)=DNUM/DEN
      WRITE(6,704)K,RLAG(K)
  704 FORMAT(1X,5H LAG%I3,3X,3H R%F6.3)
  716 CONTINUE
      ISCALE=1
      N=1
      M=JJ
      DO 650 I=1,JJ
  650 XX(I,1)=RLAG(I)
      CALL PLOT(M,N,ISCALE,XX,FNAM)
  804 CONTINUE
      RETURN
      END
```

```
      SUBROUTINE PLOT (M,N,ISCALE,XX,FNAM)
C ADAPTED FROM THE SUBROUTINE-GRAPH- OF -PERSUB- WRITTEN BY J.H.WARD,J-.
C KATHLEEN DAVIS, AND JANICE BUCHHORN,LACKLAND AIR FORCE BASE,TEXAS
C ADAPTED FOR FORTRAN II BY T.O.MAGUIRE,UNIVERSITY OF ILLINOIS
      DIMENSION RAT(10),FND(5,10),ENCRMT(10),PA(120),FMT(3),PB(10)
      DIMENSION XX(200,10),AMAX(10),AMIN(10),B(10),FNAM(5,5),BB(10)
      DATA BB(1),BB(2),BB(3),BB(4),BB(5),BB(6),BB(7),BB(8),BB(9),BB(10)/
     11H1,1H5,1HD,1H5,1H1,1HO,1HX,1HW,1HH,1HA/
      DATA PCROSS,PBLANK,PDASH,PERIOD/1H*,1H ,1H-,1H./
      DATA FMT(1),FMT(2),FMT(3)/1H ,1H0,1H-/
      IF(N-5)200,201,200
  201 DO 276 I=1,5
  276 B(I)=BB(I)
      GO TO 202
  200 DO 277 I=1,3
      II=I+5
  277 B(I)=BB(II)
  202 CONTINUE
   99 FMS=FMT(ISCALE-1)
   98 DO 100 I=1,N
      AMIN(I)=+1.E+37
  100 AMAX(I)=-1.E+37
C SEARCH FOR MAXIMA AND MINIMA
      ABMIN=AMIN(1)
      ABMAX=AMAX(1)
      DO 101 I=1,M
      DO 101 J=1,N
      COMP=XX(I,J)-AMIN(J)
      IF(COMP)4002,4003,4003
 4002 AMIN(J)=XX(I,J)
 4003 COMP=XX(I,J)-AMAX(J)
      IF(COMP)101,101,4004
 4004 AMAX(J)=XX(I,J)
  101 CONTINUE
      IF(N-5)250,251,250
  251 DO 252 J=1,5
      AMAX(J)=AMAX(5)
  252 AMIN(J)=AMIN(1)
  250 CONTINUE
      N1=N
      DO 108 J=1,N
C COMPUTE RESOLUTION OF GRAPH
  108 RAT(J)=(AMAX(J)-AMIN(J))/110.
      DO 110   J=1,N
      ENCRMT(J)=(AMAX(J)-AMIN(J))/4.
      FND(1,J)=AMIN(J)+.05
      COMP=AMIN(J)
      IF(COMP)4005,4006,4006
 4005 FND(1,J)=FND(1,J)-.10
 4006 FND(5,J)=AMAX(J)-.05
      COMP=AMAX(J)
      IF(COMP)4007,4008,4008
C PREPARE ORDINATE LABELS
 4007 FND(5,J)=FND(5,J)-.10
 4008 FND(2,J)=AMIN(J)+ENCRMT(J)+.05
      COMP=FND(2,J)
      IF(COMP)4009,4010,4010
 4009 FND(2,J)=FND(2,J)-.10
 4010 FND(3,J)=AMIN(J)+(ENCRMT(J)*2.)+.05
      COMP=FND(3,J)
      IF(COMP)4011,4012,4012
 4011 FND(3,J)=FND(3,J)-.10
 4012 FND(4,J)=AMAX(J)-ENCRMT(J)+.05
      COMP=FND(4,J)
      IF(COMP)4013,110,110
 4013 FND(4,J)=FND(4,J)-.10
  110 CONTINUE
C PRINT LEFT HAND LABELS
      WRITE(6,7)((FND(I,J),I=1,5),B(J),J=1,N1)
```

```
    7  FORMAT(///1XF6.1,21XF6.1,21XF6.1,21XF6.1,21XF6.1,3XA1)
C PLOT LEFT HAND MARGIN
       DO 4014 I=1,59
 4014 PA(I)=PDASH
       WRITE(6,8)(PA(I),I=1,59)
    8  FORMAT(1X,59A2)
       DO 140 I=1,M
       DO 4015 II=1,120
 4015 PA(II)=PBLANK
       DO 121 IX=27,81,27
  121 PA(IX)=PERIOD
       NCOMP=I
 4016 NCOMP=NCOMP-10
       IF(NCOMP)124,4017,4016
 4017 CONTINUE
       DO 123 IX=6,120,2
  123 PA(IX)=PDASH
C RESCALE DATA POINTS
  124  DO 135 K=1,N
       ZL=(XX(I,K)-AMIN(K))/RAT(K)+1.0
       L=ZL
       IF(L-1)6018,6019,6019
 6018 L=1
 6019 IF(110-L)6020,6021,6021
 6020 L=110
 6021 IF(PA(L).EQ.PBLANK)GO TO 130
       IF(PA(L).EQ.PERIOD)GO TO 130
       IF(PA(L).EQ.PDASH)GO TO 130
       PA(L)=PCROSS
       GO TO 135
  130 PB(K)=B(K)
       PA(L)=PB(K)
  135 CONTINUE
       IF(ISCALE-1)6023,136,6023
    6  FORMAT(A1)
 6023 WRITE(6,6)FMS
C PLOT DATA POINTS
  136 WRITE(6,2)I,PERIOD,(PA(J),J=1,110),PERIOD,I
    2  FORMAT(1X,I3,A1,110A1,A1,I3)
  140 CONTINUE
       DO 6026 I=1,59
 6026 PA(I)=PDASH
       WRITE(6,8)(PA(I),I=1,59)
       WRITE(6,7)((FND(I,J),I=1,5),B(J),J=1,N1)
  142 WRITE(6,3)
    3  FORMAT(1H0,10X,16HPLOT DESCRIPTION/1H0,7X,5HTITLE,10X,9HCHARACTER,
      14X,7HMINIMUM,4X,7HMAXIMUM,4X,10HRESOLUTION)
       DO 122 J=1,N
  122 WRITE(6,4)(FNAM(J,K),K=1,5),B(J),AMIN(J),AMAX(J),RAT(J)
    4  FORMAT(1X,5A4,2X,A1,7XF8.3,3XF8.3,4XF8.3)
       RETURN
       END




       SUBROUTINE MATINV(A,N,B,M,DETERM)
C      MATRIX INVERSION WITH ACCOMPANYING SOLUTION OF LINEAR EQUATIONS
       DIMENSION A(4,4),B(4,1),IPIVOT(4),INDEX(4,2),PIVOT(4)
       EQUIVALENCE (IROW,JROW),(ICOLUM,JCOLUM),(AMAX,T,SWAP)
C      INITIALIZATION
   10  DETERM=1.0
   15  DO 20 J=1,N
   20  IPIVOT(J)=0
   30  DO 550 I=1,N
C      SEARCH FOR PIVOT ELEMENT
   40  AMAX=0.0
   45  DO 105 J=1,N
   50  IF (IPIVOT(J)-1) 60,105,60
```

```
 60     DO 100 K=1,N
 70     IF (IPIVOT(K)-1) 80,100,740
 80     IF (ABS (AMAX)-ABS (A(J,K))) 85, 85, 100
 85     IROW=J
 90     ICOLUM=K
 95     AMAX=A(J,K)
100     CONTINUE
105     CONTINUE
110     IPIVOT (ICOLUM)=IPIVOT(ICOLUM)+1
C       INTERCHANGE ROWS TO PUT PIVOT ELEMENT ON DIAGONAL
130     IF(IROW-ICOLUM) 140,260,140
140     DETERM=-DETERM
150     DO 200 L=1,N
160     SWAP=A(IROW,L)
170     A(IROW,L)=A(ICOLUM,L)
200     A(ICOLUM,L)=SWAP
205     IF(M) 260,260,210
210     DO 250 L=1,M
220     SWAP=B(IROW,L)
230     B(IROW,L)=B(ICOLUM,L)
250     B(ICOLUM,L)=SWAP
260     INDEX(I,1)=IROW
270     INDEX(I,2)=ICOLUM
310     PIVOT(I)=A(ICOLUM,ICOLUM)
320     DETERM=DETERM*PIVOT(I)
        IF(PIVOT(I)) 330,720,330
C       DIVIDE PIVOT ROW BY PIVOT ELEMENT
330     A(ICOLUM,ICOLUM)=1.0
340     DO 350 L=1,N
350     A(ICOLUM,L)=A(ICOLUM,L)/PIVOT(I)
355     IF(M) 380,380,360
360     DO 370 L=1,M
370     B(ICOLUM,L)=B(ICOLUM,L)/PIVOT(I)
C       REDUCE NON-PIVOT ROWS
380     DO 550 L1=1,N
390     IF(L1-ICOLUM) 400,550,400
400     T=A(L1,ICOLUM)
420     A(L1,ICOLUM)=0.0
430     DO 450 L=1,N
450     A(L1,L)=A(L1,L)-A(ICOLUM,L)*T
455     IF(M) 550,550,460
460     DO 500 L=1,M
500     B(L1,L)=B(L1,L)-B(ICOLUM,L)*T
550     CONTINUE
C       INTERCHANGE COLUMNS
600     DO 710 I=1,N
610     L=N+1-I
620     IF(INDEX(L,1)-INDEX(L,2)) 630,710,630
630     JROW=INDEX(L,1)
640     JCOLUM=INDEX(L,2)
650     DO 705 K=1,N
660     SWAP=A(K,JROW)
670     A(K,JROW)=A(K,JCOLUM)
700     A(K,JCOLUM)=SWAP
705     CONTINUE
710     CONTINUE
        RETURN
720     WRITE (6       ,730   )
730     FORMAT (20H  MATRIX IS SINGULAR)
740     RETURN
        END
```

References

Alinsky, S. D. *Rules for radicals: A practical primer for realistic radicals.* New York: Vintage, 1971.

Allison, J., Blatt, S., & Zimet, C. N. *The interpretation of psychological tests.* New York: Harper & Row, 1968.

Archibald, R. D., & Villoria, R. L. *Network-based management systems (PERT/CPM).* New York: Wiley, 1968.

Ayllon, T., & Azrin, N. *The token economy.* New York: Appleton-Century-Crofts, 1968.

Bach, G. A., & Wyden, P. *The intimate enemy: How to fight fair in love and marriage.* New York: Harper & Row, 1968.

Bandura, A. *Psychological modeling: Conflicting theories.* Chicago: Aldine-Atherton, 1971.

Bandura, A. *Principles of behavior modification.* New York: Holt, Rinehart and Winston, 1969.

Bandura, A., & Walters, R. *Social learning and personality development.* New York: Holt, Rinehart and Winston, 1963.

Barber, T., DiCara, L., Kamiya, J., Miller, N. E., Shapiro, D., & Stoyva J. (Eds.), *Biofeedback and self-control.* Chicago: Aldine-Atherton, 1971.

Bartlett, M. S. On the theoretical specification of sampling properties of auto-correlated time-series. *Journal of the Royal Statistical Society, (Series B),* 1946, *8,* 27–47.

Bergin, A. E. The evaluation of therapeutic outcomes. In A. E. Bergin & S. L. Garfield (Eds.), *Handbook of Psychotherapy and Behavior Change.* New York: Wiley, 1971, 217–270.

Bettelheim, B. *The empty fortress: Infantile autism and the birth of the self.* New York: Free Press, 1967.

Block, J. *The Q-sort method in personality assessment and psychiatric research.* Springfield, Ill.: Charles C Thomas, 1961.

Boocock, S. J., & Schild, E. O. (Eds.), *Simulation games in learning.* Beverly Hills, Calif.: Sage Publications, 1968.

Box, G. E. P., & Jenkins, G. M. *Time series analysis: Forecasting and control.* San Francisco: Holden-Day, 1970.

Box, G.E. P., & Tiao, G. C. A change in level of a nonstationary time-series. *Biometrika*, 1965, *52*, 181–192.

Bradfield, R. H. (Ed.) *Behavior modification: The human effort.* San Rafael, Calif.: Dimensions Publishing Company, 1970.

Browning, R. M., & Stover, D. O. *Behavior modification in child treatment.* Chicago: Aldine-Atherton, 1971.

Budzynski, T., & Stoyva, J. Biofeedback techniques in behavior therapy and autogenic training. Unpublished paper, University of Colorado Medical Center, Denver, Colo., 1970.

Budzynski, T. H., Stoyva, J. M., & Adler, C. S. Feed-back-induced muscle relaxation: Application to tension head-ache. *Behavior Therapy and Experimental Psychiatry*, 1970, *1*, 205–211.

Campbell, D. T. Reforms as experiments. *American Psychologist*, 1969, *24*, 409–429.

Campbell, D. T., & Stanley, J. C. Experimental and quasi-experimental designs for research. In N. L. Gage (Ed.), *Handbook of Educational Research.* New York: Rand McNally, 1963.

Cattell, R. B., & Eber, H. N. *Handbook for the sixteen personality factors questionnaire.* Champaign, Ill.: Institute for Personality and Ability Testing (IPAT), 1957 (1964).

Cautela, J. R. Covert reinforcement. *Behavior Therapy*, 1970, *1*, 33–50.

Cautela, J. Covert sensitization. *Psychological Reports*, 1967, *20* 459–468.

Cautela, J. R. Treatment of compulsive behavior by covert sensitization. *Psychological Record*, 1966, *16*, 33–41.

Cautela, J. R., & Kastenbaum, R. A reinforcement survey schedule for use in therapy, training, and research. *Psychological Reports*, 1967, *20*, 1115–1130.

Chassan, J. B. *Research designs in clinical psychology and psychiatry.* New York: Appleton-Century-Crofts, 1967.

Cohen, A. R. *Attitude change and social influence.* New York: Basic Books, 1964.

Colby, K. M. *A primer for psychotherapists.* New York: Ronald, 1951.

Dahlstrom, W. G., & Welsh, G. S. *An MMPI Handbook.* St. Paul, Minn.: North Central Publishing Co., 1960.

Doyle, A. C. *A study in scarlet.* London: Lippincott, 1890.

Dunlap, K. *Habits, their making and unmaking.* New York: Liveright, 1932.

Edwards, A. L., & Cronbach, L. J. Experimental design for research in psychotherapy. *Journal of Clinical Psychology*, 1966, *8*, 51–59.

Ellis, A., & Harper, R. A. *A guide to rational living.* Englewood Cliffs, N.J.: Prentice-Hall, 1961.

Espich, J. E., & Williams, B. *Developing programmed instructional materials: A handbook for program writers.* Palo Alto, Calif.: Fearon Publishers, 1967.

Ferster, C. B., Nurnberger, J. I., & Levitt, E. B. The control of eating. *Journal of Mathematics*, 1962, *1*, 87–107.

Fisher, R. A. Studies in crop variation. *Journal of Agricultural Science*, 1921, *2*, 8–35.

Fitts, W. *The experience of psychotherapy*. New York: Van Nostrand Reinhold, Co., 1965.

Fox, L. Effecting the use of efficient study habits. *Journal of Mathematics,* 1962, *1*, 75–86.

Freud, A. *The psychoanalytical treatment of children*. New York: Schocken Books, 1964.

Gagné, R. M. Curriculum research and the promotion of learning. In R. E. Stake (Ed.), *AERA Curriculum Monograph Series, No. 1.* Chicago: Rand McNally, 1967.

Garfield, S. L. Research on client variables in psychotherapy. In Allen E. Bergin and Sol L. Garfield (Eds.), *Handbook of psychotherapy and behavior change*. New York: Wiley, 1971.

Gergen, K. *The psychology of behavior exchange*. Reading Mass.: Addison-Wesley, 1969.

Gerst, M. D. Symbolic coding processes in observational learning. In A. Bandura (Ed.), *Psychological Modeling: Conflicting Theories.* Chicago: Aldine-Atherton, 1971.

Glass, G. V., & Maguire, T. O. Analysis of time-series quasi-experiments. Final report, USOE, Project No. 6-8329. University of Colorado, 1968.

Glass, G. V., Willson, V. L., & Gottman, J. M. *Design and analysis of time-series experiments*. Boulder, Colo.: Laboratory of Educational Research Press, 1973.

Glasser, W. *Reality therapy: A new approach to psychiatry*. New York: Harper & Row, 1965.

Goffman, E. *The presentation of self in everyday life*. New York: Doubleday, 1959.

Goldiamond, I. Self-control procedures in personal behavior problems. *Psychological Reports,* 1965, *17*, 851–868.

Goldsmith, J. B. Systematic development and evaluation of a behavioral program for training psychiatric inpatients in interpersonal skills. Unpublished doctoral dissertation. University of Wisconsin, Madison, Wisconsin, 1973.

Goldstein, A. P. *Psychotherapeutic attraction*. New York: Pergamon, 1971.

Goldstein, A. P. *Therapist-patient expectancies in psychotherapy*. New York: Pergamon, 1962.

Goldstein, A. P., Heller, K., & Sechrest, L. B. *Psychotherapy and the psychology of behavior change*. New York: Wiley, 1966.

Gottman, J. M., N-of-one and N-of-two research in psychotherapy. *Psychological Bulletin,* 1973, *80,* No. 2, 93–105.

Gottman, J. M. Time-series analysis in the behavioral sciences and a methodology for action research. Unpublished doctoral dissertation, University of Wisconsin, 1971.

Gottman, J. M., & Asher, S. R. Modification of peer communication. Unpublished report to Madison Public Schools by the Instructional Research Laboratory, Madison, Wisconsin, 1972.

Gottman, J. M., & Clasen, R. E. *Evaluation in education: A practitioner's guide*. Itasca, Ill.: F. E. Peacock Press, 1972.

Gottman, J. M., McFall, R. M., & Barnett, J. T. Design and analysis of research using time series. *Phsychological Bulletin,* 1969, 72, No. 4, 299-306. *Clinical Psychology,* 1972, *39*, No. 2, 273–281.

Gottman, J. M., McFall, R. M., & Barnett, J. T. Design and analysis of research using time series. *Psychological Bulletin*, 1969, *72*, No. 4, 299–306.

Gough, H. G. Academic achievement in high school as predicted from the California Psychological Inventory. *Journal of Educational Psychology*, 1964, *55*, 174–180.

Grace, W. J., & Graham, D. T. Relationship of specific attitudes and emotions to certain bodily diseases. *Psychosomatic Medicine*, 1952, *14*, 243–251.

Haley, J. The art of being a failure as a therapist. *American Journal of Orthopsychiatry*, 1969, *39*, 1, 691–695.

Haley, J. *Strategies of psychotherapy*. New York: Grune & Stratton, 1963.

Harlow, H. F. The formation of learning sets. *Psychological Review*, 1949, *56*, 51–65.

Hartley, E. L., & Hartley, R. E. *Fundamentals of social psychology*. New York: Alfred A. Knopf, 1952.

Hartman, W. E., & Fithian, M. A. *Treatment of sexual dysfunction: A bio-psycho-social approach*. Long Beach, Calif.: Center for Marital and Sexual Studies, 1972.

Hendrickson, G., & Schroeder, W. H. Transfer of training in learning to hit a submerged target. *Journal of Educational Psychology*, 1941, *32*, 205–213.

Hewett, F. M. Teaching speech to an autistic child through operant conditioning. *American Journal of Orthopsychiatry*, 1965, *35*, 927–936.

Hilgard, J. R. The effect of delayed practice on memory and motor performance studied by the method of co-twin control. *Genetic Psychology Monographs*, 1933, *6*, 67.

Hoehn-Saric, R., Frank, J. D., Imber, S. D., Nash, E. H., Jr., Stone, A. R., & Battle, C. C. Systematic preparation of patients for psychotherapy. I. Effects on therapy behavior and outcome. *Journal of Psychiatric Research*, 1964, *2*, 267–281.

Hogan, R., & Kirchner, J. Preliminary report of the extinction of learned fear in a short-term implosive therapy. *Journal of Abnormal Psychology*, 1967, *72*, 106–109.

Jefferson, L. *These are my sisters*. Tulsa, Okla.: Vickers, 1948.

Judd, C. H. Practice and its effects on the perception of illusions. *Psychological Review*, 1902, *9*, 27–39.

Kanfer, F. H., & Saslow, G. Behavioral diagnosis. In C. M. Franks (Ed.), *Behavior therapy: Appraisal and status*. New York: McGraw-Hill, 1969, 417–444.

Kelly, G. A. *The psychology of personal constructs*, Vols. 1 and 2. New York: Van Nostrand Reinhold Co., 1955.

Kepka, E. J. Model representation and the threat of instability in the interrupted time-series quasi-experiment. Unpublished doctoral dissertation, Northwestern University, 1972.

Krasner, L. The psychotherapist as a social reinforcement machine. In H. H. Strupp and L. Luborsky (Eds.), *Research in psychotherapy*. Vol. II. Washington, D. C.: American Psychological Association, 1962, 61–94.

Lazarus, A. A. *Behavior therapy and beyond*. New York: McGraw-Hill, 1971.

Lazarus, A. A. Behavior therapy and graded structure. In R. Porter (Ed.), *The role of learning in psychotherapy*. Boston: Little, Brown, 1968.

Lederer, W. J., & Jackson, D. D. *The mirages of marriage.* New York: Norton, 1968.

Lehrer, G. F. J. Negative practice as a psychotherapeutic technique. In Hans Eysenck (Ed.), *Behavior therapy and the neuroses.* Oxford: Pergamon, 1960.

Leiblum, S. The effect of experimenter-observation and nonobservation, payoff and nonpayoff and mode of delivery of verbalization on adherence to instructions. Unpublished doctoral dissertation, University of Illinois, 1971.

Levy, L. *Psychological interpretation.* New York: Holt, Rinehart and Winston, 1963.

Lewin, K. The conceptual representation and measurement of psychological forces. *Contributions to psychological theory,* 1938, *1*, No. 4.

Lichstein, E. Techniques for assessing outcomes of psychotherapy. In P. McReynolds, *Advances in psychological assessment,* Vol. 2. Palo Alto, Calif.: Science and Behavior Books, 1970.

London, P. *The modes and morals of psychotherapy.* New York: Holt, Rinehart and Winston, 1964.

Lovaas, O. I., Schaeffer, B., & Simmons, J. F. Experimental studies in childhood schizophrenia: Building social behavior in autistic children by use of electric shock. *Journal of Experimental Research in Personality,* 1965, *1*, 99–109.

Mager, R. F. *Preparing instructional objectives.* Palo Alto, Calif.: Fearon Publishers, 1962.

Mahrer, A. R. *The goals of psychotherapy.* New York: Appleton-Century-Crofts, 1967.

Malott, R. W. *Contingency management in education.* Kalamazoo, Mich.: Behavioradelia Press, 1972.

Marquis, J. N., Morgan, W. G., & Piaget, G. W. *A guidebook for systematic desensitization.* Palo Alto, Calif.: Veterans' Workshop, Veterans' Administration Hospital, 1971.

Maslow, A. *Toward a psychology of being.* New York: Van Nostrand Reinhold Co., 1962.

Masters, W. H., & Johnson, V. E. *Human sexual inadequacy.* Boston: Little, Brown, 1970.

McFall, R. M. The effect of self-monitoring on normal smoking behavior. *Journal of Consulting and Clinical Psychology,* 1970, *35*, 135–142.

McFall, R. M., & Marston, A. R. An experimental investigation of behavior rehearsal, modeling, and coaching to assertion. *Journal of Abnormal Psychology,* 1970, *76*, 295–303.

McFall, R. M., & Twentyman, C. T. Four experiments on the relative contributions of rehearsal, modeling, and coaching to assertion training. *Journal of Abnormal Psychology,* 1973, *81*, No. 3, 199–218.

McReynolds, P. (Ed.) *Advances in psychological assessment,* 2 vols. Palo Alto, Calif.: Science and Behavior Books, 1970.

Meehl, P. E. *Clinical vs. statistical prediction.* Minneapolis: University of Minnesota Press, 1954.

Meltzoff, J., & Kornreich, M. *Research in psychotherapy.* New York: Aldine-Atherton, 1970.

Mischel, W. *Personality and assessment.* New York: Wiley, 1968.

Mowrer, O. H., Light, D. H., Luria, Z., & Seleny, M. P. Tension changes during psychotherapy. In O. H. Mowrer (Ed.), *Psychotherapy: Theory and research.* New York: Ronald. 1953.

Murstein, B. I. (Ed.) *Handbook of projective techniques.* New York: Basic Books, 1965.

Palkes, H., Stewart, M., & Kahana, B. Porteus maze performance of hyperactive boys after training in self-directed verbal commands. *Child Development,* 1968, *39,* 817–826.

Patterson, G. R., Cobb, J. A., & Ray, R. S. Direct intervention in the classroom: A set of procedures for the aggressive child. Paper presented at the meeting of the Third Banff Conference on Behavior Modification, April 1971. F. W. Clark, D. L. Evans, and L. A. Hamerlynck (Eds.) *Implementing behavioral programs in educational and clinical settings.* Champaign, Ill.: Research Press, 1971.

Patterson, G. R., & Guillion, M. E. *Living with children: New methods for parents and teachers.* Champaign, Ill.: Research Press, 1968.

Rachman, S., & Teasdale, J. *Aversion therapy and behavior disorders: An analysis.* Coral Gables, Fla.: University of Miami Press, 1969.

Rappaport, R. *Diagnostic psychological testing.* New York: International University Press, 1968.

Rathus, S. An experimental investigation of assertive training in a group setting. *Journal of Behavior Therapy and Experimental Psychiatry,* Vol. 3, 1972, 81–86.

Redl, F., & Wineman, D. *The aggressive child.* Glencoe, Ill.: The Free Press, 1957.

Rogers, C. R., & Dymond, R. F. *Psychotherapy and personality change.* Chicago: University of Chicago Press, 1954.

Rotter, J. B. *Social learning and clinical psychology.* Englewood Cliffs, N.J.: Prentice-Hall, 1954.

Rowntree, D. *Basically branching: A handbook for programmers.* London: MacDonald Press, 1966.

Salter, A. *Conditioned reflex therapy.* New York: Farrar, Strauss, 1949.

Satir, V. A. *Conjoint family therapy.* Palo Alto, Calif.: Science and Behavior Books, 1964.

Schaefer, H., Sobell, M., & Mills, K. Baseline drinking behaviors in alcoholics and social drinkers' kinds of drinks and sip magnitudes. *Behavior Research and Therapy,* 1971, *9,* 23–27.

Schofield, W. The structured personality inventory in measurement of effects of psychotherapy. In L. A. Gottschalk & A. H. Averback (Eds.), *Methods of research in psychotherapy.* New York: Appleton-Century-Crofts, 1966, 536–550.

Schutz, W. C. *Joy: Expanding human awareness.* New York: Grove Press, 1967.

Schwitzgebel, R., & Kolb, D. A. Inducing behavior change in adolescent delinquents. *Behavior Research and Therapy,* 1964, *1,* 297–304.

Schwitzgebel, R., & Schwitzgebel, R. Reduction of adolescent crime by a research method. *Journal of Social Therapy,* 1961, 7, 212–215.

Sechrest, L. B., & Strowig, R. W. Teaching machines and the individual learner. *Educational Therapy,* 1962, *12,* 157–169.

Shewart, W. A. *Economic control of quality of manufactured product*. New York: Van Nostrand Reinhold Co., 1931.

Skinner, B. F. *Beyond freedom and dignity*. New York: Alfred A. Knopf, 1971.

Slack, C. W. Experimenter-subject psychotherapy: A new method of introducing intensive office treatment for unreachable cases. *Mental Hygiene*, 1960, *44*, 238-256.

Stampfl, T. G., & Levis, D. J. Essentials of implosive therapy: A learning theory based on psychodynamic behavioral therapy. *Journal of Abnormal Psychology*, 1967, *72*, 496-503.

Stollak, G. E., & Guerney, B., Jr. Exploration of personal problems by juvenile delinquents under conditions of minimal reinforcement. *Journal of Clinical Psychology*, 1964, *20*, 283-297.

Stone, P. Personal problem solving for clients in a university psychological clinic. Unpublished clinic guide, Indiana University Psychological Clinic, 1972.

Stuart, R. B. *Slim chance in a fat world*. Champaign, Ill.: Research Press, 1972.

Sullivan, H. S. *The psychiatric interview*. New York: Norton, 1954.

Sullivan, H. S. *The interpersonal theory of psychiatry*. New York: Norton, 1953.

Tate, B. G., & Baroff, G. S. Aversive control of self-injurious behavior in a psychotic boy. *Behavior Research Therapy*, 1966, *4*, 281-287.

Todd, F. J., & Kelley, R. J. Behavior complexity, behavior analysis and behavior therapy. Unpublished paper, University of Colorado Medical Center, 1972.

Ullmann, L. P., & Krasner, L. (Eds.) *Case studies in behavior modification*. New York: Holt, Rinehart and Winston, 1965.

Ulmer, G. Teaching geometry to cultivate reflective thinking: An experimental study with 1239 high school pupils. *Journal of Experimental Education*, 1939, *8*, 18-25.

Urban, H. B., & Ford, D. H. Some historical and conceptual perspectives on psychotherapy and behavior change. In A. E. Bergin and S. L. Garfield (Eds.), *Handbook of psychotherapy and behavior change*. New York: Wiley, 1971, 3-35.

Wallerstein, R. S. The goals of psychoanalysis. A survey of analytic viewpoints. *Journal of the American Psychoanalytic Association*, 1965, *13*, 743-770.

Webb, E., Campbell, D., Schwartz, R., & Sechrest, L. *Unobtrusive measures: Non-reactive research in the social sciences*. Chicago: Rand McNally, 1966.

Wilkins, W. Desensitization: Social and cognitive factors influencing the effectiveness of Wolpe's procedure. *Psychological Bulletin*, 1971, *76*, 311-317.

Wolberg, L. R. *The technique of psychotherapy*. New York: Grune & Stratton, 1954.

Wolpe, J., & Lazarus, A. A. *Behavior therapy techniques*. New York: Pergamon, 1966.

Woodrow, H. The effect of type of training upon transference. *Journal of Educational Psychology*, 1927, *18*, 159-172.

AUTHOR INDEX

SUBJECT INDEX